FORTUNE FAVORS THE BOLD

Volume one

The SAGA of the SCISSORWULF

Fortune Favors the Bold volume one: the Saga of the Scissorwulf
and everything in it
© 2016 Chad Derdowski
All Rights Reserved

In days of long ago, in a time before time, when wizards and warriors walked the earth and meddling gods still mingled in the matters of mortals...

A time when champions clashed and games of war were waged on verdant fields of battle. This is a time of dragons and marvelous beasts. A time of magic and witchcraft. This is a time of steel. This is the time of the Scissorwulf!

But be wary, adventurer, should you choose to walk the path of the warrior, for such a journey is not to be taken lightly. The path you will follow is yours and yours alone. As such, the pages of this tome are not to be read in order; rather, follow the instructions you will find at the bottom of each page. 'Tis a long and winding road and every decision you make shall affect the telling of the tale.

Good luck, dear reader and remember – Fortune Favors the Bold!

Turn to page 4.

Hidden by the dark of night, Ookla and Thaarl finished the remainder of their dinner in silence, alone save for the watchful eye of the gibbous moon, which hung in the sky like a pregnant grapefruit. A myriad of insects and woodland creatures offered a gentle chorus to accompany their meal. After traveling many leagues, the two thieves' journey was nearly at its end. Tomorrow morning, they would reach the nearby city of Gran'daven and meet with their contact to exchange the precious cargo they'd been carrying for gold.

Gold! And with it, the promise of mead, a well cooked meal, a warm bed and the comfort of a whore's loins. 'Twas the sea merchants of Prown who had long ago coined the phrase "Any port in a storm" and both Ookla and Thaarl had found this particular bit of wisdom to hold true. But both men had grown weary of calloused hands and rotten teeth upon their member and longed for the velvet embrace of a woman's nethers.

But tomorrow was in the realm of dreams and tonight called for celebration. As such, Ookla called for a rather unusual after dinner treat.

"Thaarl, my friend, our long journey nears its end and I propose that we celebrate by sampling some of our employers wares. Surely, a small bit will go unnoticed!"

As he spoke, Ookla reached into his steed's leather saddle and produced in one hand, a small earthen bowl and in the other – the fabled horn of the unicorn, long thought to be lost to the mists and legends of time, if indeed it ever existed at all!

And yet, here it was. And what shall he do with it?

Turn to page 5 to find out!

Placing the horn in the bowl, Ookla applied pressure and began to turn the horn in a clockwise rotation. Soon, a fine powder began to flake off of the antler. When a sufficient amount coated the bottom of the bowl, Ookla returned the horn to its resting place in his horse's saddle.

Thaarl watched with hungry eyes as Ookla reached inside his shirt to retrieve a tiny silver spoon that hung about his neck on a thin chain. Shoveling the tiniest bit of the powder onto the spoon, Ookla first offered it to his companion, who eagerly inhaled, before repeating the process and imbibing his own.

Crouched behind a thorny shrub, you watch these sights unfold with a steely-eyed gaze. You have travelled this road for some time now, following these brigands for so long, you almost feel as though you are a part of their band. Yet this atrocity is but the latest in a long string of vile acts and your blood begins to boil.

You – the Scissorwulf! Friend of nature and self-appointed Doler of Justice. You are your own spirit animal and naught brings you pleasure like relieving the shoulders of those who would do evil the burden of carrying their heads. No fucks asked; none given.

Will you act upon said rage? Turn to page 6.

Or should you wait it out and follow these thieves to their destination and perhaps a greater prize? Turn to page 9

"What was that noise?" Thaarl hissed, jerking his head from side to side, scanning the darkened landscape with bloodshot eyes.

"I heard something out there!"

"'Twas naught but your imagination, fool!" Ookla scolded him, "Perhaps I should've thought better than to offer you a snort! Thou are but a lightweight!"

Before Ookla could continue to admonish his companion, he found himself gasping for air as a broadsword – your broadsword – entered his ribcage and protruded though his chestal region, propelled by the unearthly power of your sinewy muscles.

Turning to see his cohort's lifeless body slumped on the forest floor, surrounded by an ever-growing pool of blood, Thaarl's voice was little more than a whisper.

"Who – who's there?"

Recognizing the power of the moment, you decide to make your entrance. Stepping from the darkness of the forest glen into the light of the silvery moon, you announce your presence, as is the custom of your people.

"I am the shadow which emerges from darkness, the Keeper of the Extinguished Flame. I am fury! I am vengeance! I am The Scissorwulf!"

Shit is about to go down on page 8.

You learn a great number of things over the span of a few hours and many questions asked. You learn that the voice in your head is an artificial computer brain which had been placed there to control your actions when needed, and offer guidance when you were trusted to function on your own (or when a lack of regular repair resulted in your normal human brain coming online again. Oh, and you learned what "online" meant too). As it turns out, you've been an alien-fightin' cyborg warrior for over 40 years and the formula for creating another time machine was lost in the war, so you can't go home. But there's good news! The battery inside you will keep your robotic heart beating for at least another 275 million years, so you're cool to keep doing this pretty much forever.

And that big ol' robot brain of yours? As the repository of all recorded human history prior to the alien invasion, so if you wanted to just keep asking questions and learn everything there is to know, you could conceivably do so. Except for how to build another time machine; that's the one bit of information that was lost. Sorry.

A wave of depression washes over you. Everything and everyone you know and love is gone and you are trapped in a world you never made – never even imagined! Looking at it logically, (as someone with a robot brain is wont to do), you realize you have two options:

You could just find a really high cliff and jump off. That would probably smash up all your robot parts as well as mangling the shit out of what's left of your human parts.

But if that's your attitude, then why don't you just close this fucking book right now, you fucking quitter. Seriously, close it and put it back on your shelf. Or give it to someone else; someone who gives a damn. Because frankly, you don't even deserve to live vicariously through the Scissorwulf and his many exciting adventures, you fucking asshole.

Or you could keep on keepin' on and turn to page 103. Like the real goddamn Scissorwulf would do.

You can't be sure that Thaarl heard your speech in its entirety, given that his shrill screams, not unlike those of a child, filled the air from the moment you made yourself known and did not cease until he turned away to run, only to trip over a root and find himself sprawled upon the ground.

Mounting him as a lion might mount its mate, you grab a handful of hair and press the cold steel of your sword – still sticky with Ookla's blood - against his neck. If you harbored any doubts about whether or not he took you seriously, the rank stench of Thaarl's urine fills the forest air, as if to mark his territory. Putting your mouth directly next to his ear, you speak...

"What is your business here, knave? What manner of rapscallion traffics in the sale of the horny horse's horn? Speak true, for the Widowmaker can sense a lie!"

His face a mask of snot and tears, Thaarl manages to squeak out a reply between sobs.

"We was just mules, sir! Supposed to deliver the package to our contact in Gran'daven tomorrow! We was supposed to meet at the Regal Beagle at noon sharp!"

You've learned all there is to know and Thaarl is no longer of use to you. Whatever shall you do with him?

If you choose to slay him, turn to page 10.

If you let him live, turn to page 11.

Born in blood and fire, your surliness is your calling card. It is said that the heart of a beast pulses within the chest of the Scissorwulf. But on this day, it is your human intellect and ability to reason which governs your soul. On this day, you choose to wait, knowing that by following these rogues to their destination, you will learn the identity of their true master and thusly discover and deliver justice to those who would desiccate the sanctity and harmony of magic and nature.

You sleep with one eye open, lest the sound of your nocturnal growling shake the trees and awaken your enemies. When day breaks, the two bandits mount up and head toward the village of Gran'daven, a shipping town known as both a port of trade and a purlieu of turpitude, where one can obtain anything one desires, be it legal, moral or otherwise.

Ookla and Thaarl are mounted on steeds, but your knowledge of the wood is unmatched by any save The Venturian himself. It will pose no challenge to beat them into town. You overheard them discussing their meeting place whilst in their narcotized stupor and intend to arrive before they do, so that you might lay in wait to spring your trap.

But we'll skip the part about all the travelling since the town is only a few minutes away and nothing particularly impressive happens. Just go ahead and turn to page 18 to find out what happens next!

"May your gods grant you the mercy that I can not." you say to Thaarl as you draw your blade across his neck. This is the custom farewell of your people and though you follow no code, it does you well to observe and remember the ancient gods and praxis.

But instead of the steady cascade of blood you expect to fall from Thaarl's neck like a crimson waterfall onto the woodland sod, you are shocked to see a rainbow of multicolored light beaming from your incision!

Stumbling backward in disbelief, your heel finds a stray rock which sends you tumbling ass over teakettle onto your posterior. Thaarl rises before you, the gaping hole in his neck pouring forth a beam of light which nearly blinds you. His hands go to his neck and prodding fingers find their way inside. Peeling his flesh off and casting it aside like so much soiled clothing, Thaarl reveals his true form as a being of pure light!

What the fuck? Turn to page 44.

Standing, you return The Widowmaker to her resting place and address your enemy.

"You may take your leave in the morning, but it shall be without your wares. I would advise haste, and a journey away from your intended destination, for your employers will surely not grant you the mercy that I have shown tonight. Do not give me cause to regret my decision."

But as you turn to walk away, you suspect what Thaarl will do. And he does not disappoint. Before you can step thrice, Thaarl has pulled a dagger from his boot! A thin smile crosses your face as you hear the familiar whoosh of air that accompanies a throwing dirk as it slices through the air toward you. Turning, you dodge the projectile, and in one swift motion you pluck the blade from the air by its handle and return the weapon to its owner. Thaarl accepts the shank with a sickening thunk as it embeds in his right thigh.

You're going to enjoy this.

Turn to page 20 for the aftermath.

You awaken lying naked on a cold slab of stone, shackles about your hands and feet. The moon hangs full above you, illuminating the grisly scene which takes place all around.

Several bonfires blaze radiantly while your captors surround you and remove the shadowy raiment that helped to obscure their form from view earlier this evening. Supple breasts and curvy hips reveal your captors to be not men, but women – women in the prime of their physical lives. You faintly recall a lesson learned about the result of making assumptions, but the memory never fully forms as you are overcome by sheer terror.

Your mind is still clouded by the lingering effects of the poison, but you swear that the moon glows ever brighter as the satchel containing the unicorn horns is produced and each woman takes one for herself. Seated in a circle around you, they begin to chant in unison. Being elevated, your view of the ritual is obscured, but as their arms move rhythmically and their chanting intensifies, the moon and bonfires respond in kind. The chanting turns to moaning and eventually shrieking and you come to realize that you have stumbled into the path of a coven of witches!

You hold on to the hope that you are to be a part of a benevolent lovemaving ritual with a congregation of amicable sorceresses, and when one of the seductresses mounts your prone form, her breasts smeared in blood and wearing a severed goat's head upon her own, your fear subsides – you can definitely get down with some kinky shit. Your manhood rises to the occasion and to your delight, she takes it inside her lubricated love canal. But when the enchantress raises a glimmering unicorn antler above her head and fiercely thrusts it into your chest, splintering your ribcage and plunging deep into your heart, you realize that this is...

THE END.

"Fuck this shit" you exclaim as you vault over the edge of the cart and race into the forest. "You're on your own now, Klaus!"

Sprinting away from the trail, you make your way toward a nearby thicket. The sound of your heart beating fills your ears, but it is not enough to drown out the incessant cries of the winged avengers seeking to destroy your companion. Soon Klaus' screams provide a counter harmony.

Is it pity that causes you to turn around, or just a morbid curiosity? Whatever the reason, the result is the same – a hideous vision that immediately sears itself into your brain, creating a memory upon your soul that shall not soon be forgotten.

Klaus' overturned cart has fallen atop his body, pinning him to the ground and making him easy prey for the birds that peck at his flesh, leaving him a bloody mess. As two crows fight over the remains of his left eye, you briefly consider Ghastly Carol's fate – an eye for an eye?

But this is no time for levity. You have never been one to let any creature suffer and you still have a chance to save this old nut. Will you accept the challenge and turn to page 67?

No, Klaus' fate is his own and he cast the die that led him to this stage of the game. Turn instead to page 78 to let him reap the harvest of the seeds he has sown.

A sense of impending doom overtakes you as the Cocktopus struggles to tear the Lady Fingerle's Revenge apart. By now, all of its gigantic, slippery limbs hold the ship in sway and edge ever closer to rupturing the integrity of the hull. But this is not the first sense of impending doom you'd been overtaken by and you have no intention of it being the last.

Gripping the Widowmaker with both hands, you begin to strike at the beast again and again, hoping it will release its grip. Mermonkeys begin to pour over the ship like water and by now, greatly outnumber her crew. Screams mingle with the sounds of breaking bones and tearing flesh.

The Cocktopus barely seems to register your assault and indeed, its hide is tougher than that of a Schlovingian hedge rhino. You hadn't realized that you were screaming, but your cries bring a rain of mermonkeys down upon you.

It is said that human toenails are a delicacy to the mermonkey and indeed, that is what they go for first. The pain is terrible but you have a point to prove, so you continue your assault on the Cocktopus. However, every delicacy must be followed by dessert and being without legs, the mermonkeys opt next for the proverbial low hanging fruit of your exposed genitals.

Do you even want to turn to page 105?

You overheard the rogues discuss their meeting place last night, a tavern known as the Regal Beagle. Arriving early, you take up residency in a corner near the back, allowing you full breadth of the comings and goings within the establishment. It doesn't take long for Ookla and Thaarl to arrive and it takes even less time for the two knaves to begin imbibing what passes for mead in this rat infested shit hole.

You pass the time sitting cross-armed and looking churlish, a tactic which serves well to dissuade any casual conversation or potential threat. Soon enough, you will have the information you require to continue your quest.

Or will you? It seems that Ookla's hands have found themselves upon the posterior of the barmaid, who happens to be the wife of a very large villager with even larger friends who happen to be seated at the next table. Fisticuffs ensue and soon it seems that nearly every patron of the tavern is involved.

But are you? Shall you offer protection to Ookla and Thaarl, so that you might later find the greater evil and dole out a mighty justice as only you can? If so, head over to page 22.

Or shall you sit back and enjoy the entertainment? You've never been one to turn down a show and this one can be found on page 72.

CRACK! The sounds of a gigantic sea creature tearing a ship apart are somehow comforting by now. It is said that in death, one's life flashes before one's eyes and you find yourself drifting slowly back to your childhood, and a memory of cutting lumber for firewood. By now, your body is covered in mermonkeys who, with no extremities left to dine upon, have moved from fingers and toes onto your proboscis and earlobes.

You marvel at the how long it takes for a ship to sink. It's been several minutes now since it was rent in two, but peering through the myriad of mermonkey faces which obfuscate your view, you can see that Lady Fingerle's Revenge is not yet halfway submerged. It is of little consequence, as it will all be over soon enough.

Your mind begins to clear. The pain slips away and even though you know your body sinks beneath the murky depths, you feel lighter, almost weightless. Darkness envelops you – a veil of the purest blackness you have ever experienced. It seems to wrap its embrace not just around your body, but your very soul.

And suddenly, a pinprick of light appears in the distance. Energized, you feel it call to you!

Will you muster what strength you have left and attempt to swim toward it? If so, turn to page 113.

Do you even have arms and legs anymore? It ain't happenin'. Turn instead to page 123 to become one with the eternal darkness.

Your first instinct is to run.

"Your attempt at escape is futile." the voice informs you, but you try anyway, making a mad dash for the doorway you'd spotted moments before. You're nearly there when a jolt of pain reverberates through your entire body, sending you to your knees. The voice which seems to come from nowhere and everywhere at once continues to address you.

"You didn't answer my question. Do you like your new body? Or should I say – MY new body? For you shall come to find that no matter how hard you try, you cannot resist my commands. Any attempt to do so will leave you feeling much like you do right now."

"I have no idea quite how you got yourself in the state you were in when I found you – the legends make no mention of your death," the disembodied voice continues, "nevertheless, I was quite pleased that my Time Scavengers discovered you on one of their routine jaunts through the timestream. And now, a bit of cybernetic reconstruction later, here we are: the legendary Scissorwulf, child of the gods and the mightiest warrior known to humankind, is in my control. And with your battle prowess and my technology combined, nothing will stand in my path of total domination!"

You don't know what the fuck is going on or what the fuck this guy is talking about. Maybe letting him go on a little more will enlighten you? Turn to page 80 to keep listening.

Fuck that shit. You are a warrior to the very core of your being and whenever you're confused, it usually means someone is trying to get the upper hand on you. Why not cut this audacious cretin's tongue from his mouth? Go for it by turning to page 57.

'Twas no more than a league to Gran'daven and as expected, forgoing the primitive roads which led to the village and travelling as the crow flies through wood and dale ensures that the hunter arrives before his prey.

Nestled in the bed of the Remulite River, the city of Gran'daven was one of the oldest cities in all of Grappleheim and recognized by civilized man as one of the largest. Settled by the Remulites, a cult of sea worshippers who also managed to get the river named after them, Gran'daven grew as quickly as that ancient religion had died out. Being a prominent shipping port with direct access to the oceans, Gran'daven was known as much for commerce as it was for crime.

Corruption had found its way into every corner of the metropolis and what had once been known as "the Golden Municipality" had become every bit as rotten as those who inhabited it. Paved streets were cracked and unrepaired. Police were easily convinced to look the other way if gold or flesh was offered, and nearly every building was in a state of perpetual disrepair.

The public waste system, however, was in pristine condition – mainly because the sewers served as a perfect means of clandestine travel or hasty escape. But that's neither here nor there.

Turn now to page 15, dear reader, and let the journey continue!

"Fuck this shit" you mutter under your breath as you reach for the sword slung about your back. The same sword you retrieved from the fiery innards of a blazing volcano after nearly losing it in a battle with the dreaded Lazer Bane. The accursed sword which lay broken and unloved, wrapped in a sheep's bladder and cast aside for the better part of a century before it sang to you in a dream, bidding you to forge it anew and reclaim the glory it knew in ancient times. The sword has lived up to its name time and again, bringing doom to those who would dare stand against the justice doled out by the mighty warrior who wields her. The sword whose true origins remained unknown to all but itself, shrouded in mystery and bathed in enigma, The Widowmaker has served you better than any friend or companion and remained more true than any lover you've known.

Ghastly Carol, aware of the almost imperceptible change left in the wake of such a divine weapon parting the molecules of air as it was awakened from its slumber, recoils and attacks in turn! You should've known better and the fraction of a second spent in reflection of your glorious weapon shall be your undoing.

So many questions left unanswered. So many quests unquested. You aren't even sure how Ghastly Carol had done you in, it had happened so fast. The one thing you are certain of, as the world around you fades to black, is that the most precious of all blades is now in the hands of your killer, who raises it above her head and brings it down upon you with a sickening THUNK!

For you, this is...

Several hours later, when your rage has subsided and the bodies have been disposed of, you sit by the edge of a blazing campfire, carefully cleaning the blood from your sword. Once again, The Widowmaker had served you well. You reflect upon her perfect steel and fondly remember the old man who had given her to you and trained you in the use of her power - the old man who had raised you when no one else gave a damn.

Returning your weapon to its sheath, you cast your eyes downward. A quick survey of the thieves' former encampment reveals a small ceramic bowl that had so captured the thieves' attention before your fatal strike. And contained within the bowl rests the powdery white substance that had raised your ire.

The fabled solitary antler of the mystical unicorn! If the old crones and fortune tellers were to be believed, such a creature hadn't been seen in over a generation. Could it be?

A quick dip of your pinky into the bowl reveals a dust clinging to your little finger. Running the digit along the length of your upper gum gives way to a tingling sensation and numbness. Whatever sorcery this is, it would no doubt provide the perfect end to an evening filled with slaying.

Shall you have a toot? Turn to page 56.

Perhaps such bedazzlement is better left alone? Turn instead to page 109 and leave well enough alone.

And what have we here? A time outside of time, a life lived in between the drops of rain. A divergence from the sacred path has brought you here, for no trails or tracts lead to such a destination. And the prize for such ingenuity is another tale within a tale.

A tale of the Gods of Old, whose kingdoms and territories were overtaken by one who would usurp their seats at the Table of the Gods and crown himself Victorious King Mayhem. It is said that the history books are written by those who sing songs of battle and walk away triumphant – and so, Victorious King Mayhem had free reign to put the pen of history to the parchment of time.

From the ground bones of the Old Gods did King Mayhem create Grappleheim and within it, The Garden, where champions and titans did battle. The new king wore an enchanted belt bedecked with the finest gold and inset with a myriad of magical gems and jewels. The belt granted him immortality and stole a measure of his soul. But the belt was cursed, and anyone who saw it lusted after its power and its promise of life eternal – a seat among the pantheon of the gods.

Knowing that he could not keep the belt, but not wanting it to fall into enemy hands, Victorious King Mayhem sowed his seed, to ensure that his lineage was strong and could maintain a grasp on such a prize. Traveling far and wide, Victorious King Mayhem used charms and glamour to lay with the New Mother Nature and learn of Sister Golden Hair's surprise. Many were the gardens of the goddesses who bore his fruit – some fine and some rotten. It is said that he even lay with the unspeakable daemons of parts unknown to further propagate his line. So it was that the Titans of Grappleheim came to be.

But lo, even the goddesses of antiquity are like the crackling of dry leaves in the autumn breeze when compared to the beauty of humankind. And when Victorious King Mayhem saw a mortal woman who set his heart to beating, he took the form of a peacock to woo her and win her love.

And it is said that the child she bore was unlike any other mortal. And as was the custom of the people of her tribe, the sacred herbs were consulted and the child was to be given the name of its spirit animal. But the name revealed in the mists of the holy smoke was that of the child itself... the Scissorwulf.

A quick headcount reveals a gang of five ruffians. It's nearly noon, so they're already fairly soused. This is going to be easy. In fact, it's likely you shan't need to awaken The Widowmaker from her place of slumber, nestled upon your muscled back. It would be a shame to deprive these men of the sound of her sweet song of steel, but perhaps it is for the best – it is oft more desirable to leave a trail of broken bones than one of blood and bodies in your wake. No need to draw any unwanted attention from the locals.

Overturning your table, you leap into action and join the fracas. Dropkicking the first thug directly in his chest, you hear a satisfying crunch that can only mean his breastbone has been shattered. You've landed on the ground, so it's easy to trip the next ruffian. When he hits the ground, a well-placed elbow ensures he won't be getting up again. A quick kip-up puts you back on your feet and directly in the path of a 370-pound roughneck with a neck as thick as your chest. His fist nearly finds your face, but you manage to duck and use his momentum against him, tossing the brute over the bar and into the realms of slumber.

When the two remaining hooligans turn tail and run, you assume it is due to the astonishing fighting prowess on display, but the hush that has fallen over the tavern and the eyes cast toward the door tell you otherwise.

Turn to page 25 to find out what's what!

23

Come the fuck on. You're barreling through a deadly forest on a rickety old wooden cart being pulled by two decrepit reindeer at an unimaginable speed, sitting next to a crazy old wizard and being chased by a flock of killer birds. Oh, and you just discovered unicorns are real.

And you're concerned about holding another man's hand? Grow the fuck up and turn to page 51. Don't give the Scissorwulf a bad name with your intolerance.

Asshole.

Agony and ecstasy become one as Asbjorn roughly turns you over and bestrides your herculean frame. This time, it would be the daemon's lady parts that would bring about your despoilment. With all the grace and grip of a coal miner's glove, the hellion's womanhood brought you to climax within moments, leaving your member raw and chafed, not unlike a cob of corn recently shucked, except a little bloody. This copulation was not simply for pleasure... no, the eerie smile which crossed the Asbjorn's misshapen lips belied the knowledge that even now, a child grew within it's rancid belly.

The gestation period of a human/daemon hybrid is remarkably short and in the course of an afternoon, Asbjorn tells you the tale of how s/he had manipulated a series of burglars, thieves and miscreants to obtain the unicorn horns long believed lost to the sands of time. Said magicks enabled the creature to manipulate time and space and bring you here, to the realm of daemons in order to make the foul, evil love which will result in the half-breed fruit of your loins.

The child would possess powers and abilities far beyond even Asbjorn's hideous imagination and indeed, would be the pre-incarnation of your daemon molester. Upon the spawn's birth, Asbjorn's essence would pass to its child and an unspeakable evil would be created.

As the sun sets and night divides the day, you play midwife and watch as the soul passed from mother to daughter/son; for your child, like that which bore it, also bears the loins of both male and female.

And you, the once proud and mighty Scissorwulf, whose soul and psyche are shattered beyond all recognition, will play nursemaid to the child that shall one day bring about the ruination of humankind and rend the heavens asunder. Every night, as you cry yourself to sleep, you pray for a death that never comes.

For you, this is the beginning; but to save our reader from horrors even more unspeakable, this must be THE END.

An almost eerie silence has fallen over the barroom. For a moment, time seems to stand still. All eyes (those that aren't swollen shut) are on the door, so you figure it's probably a good time to turn around and see just what's going on.

Your vision comes to rest upon the huge frame filling the doorway. The simple robes hide the features of the wearer, but your keen eyes would recognize the cloak of an Altazzarrian pirate and most likely, the contact Ookla and Thaarl are here to meet. It's a good thing you haven't been imbibing any spirits, as you'll need your wits about you. Altazzarrians are known for being as deadly as they are beautiful.

Removing her hood, you immediately recognize the figure in the doorway as Ghastly Carol, known far and wide as the fiercest of Altazzarrian pirates. A scar ran from forehead to chin, crossing her left eye, which was covered by an eye patch – the lone blemish on an otherwise flawless face. She stood 6'5", every inch a woman. Casting her lone eye upon you, a question crossed Ghastly Carol's perfect lips.

"Are these assholes with you?"

Well, are they? If you should choose to claim them, turn now to page 30.

Oh, hell no! Turn to page 102.

The daemon is moving closer and you're running out of time! Luckily, this particular daemon is all about the drama, otherwise it would've just killed you; but it is clearly more interesting in being all showy and making you sweat it out. Furthering the effectiveness of the goblin's dramatic overtures is your realization that it carries a bloodied unicorn horn in each clawed hand! Recognizing that shit is, indeed, about to get real, you prepare yourself for...

ATTACK! Before you know it, the monster is upon you, a hideous mass of teeth and brawn breathing heavy and dripping with saliva. Taking a step back, you instinctively raise the unbreakable enchanted steel of The Widomaker between you and the creature, as though it were a shield.

Miraculously, the daemon pauses, transfixed by it's own reflection in your sword! You have found the secret of its defeat! Relaxing, you ask the daemon from whence it came and the whys are wherefores of the predicament you find yourselves in.

The malignant spirit reveals its true name as Sacriphisto and explains that as a result of transgressions against its masters, it has been trapped between the daemon realms of magick and the mortal world in an immaterial state for nigh on seven centuries. In its travels, the creature came upon the long lost stronghold of a dead necromancer who had in his possession the only unicorn horns known to exist.

Able to influence the weak of mind, Sacriphisto has been manipulating a variety of thieves, grave robbers, treasure hunters and traffickers in illegalities in the theft of long lost antlers so that their divine power might be used to increase his might, so that he could one day trade places with a mortal soul and regain physical form.

The exploits of the Scissorwulf are known far and wide. As such, Sacriphisto sought you as a suitable candidate. But you proved too wily for the daemon and now you have discovered the hellion's fatal weakness – its own reflection!

Turn now to page 120, and let the adventure live on!

PLOP! Klaus' head falls to the ground and rolls several feet before coming to a rest on top of an anthill. Within seconds, it is covered by a swarm of Lalondian fire ants, who quickly gormandize upon the severed dome. For no sooner did the King of Birds speak did you acted, unsheathing the Widowmaker and severing Klaus' neck. Your time spent walking the warrior's path has taught you to trust but two things in life: your sword and your gut. And every word the King of Birds said rang with the sound of truth's bell.

As did the rest of Klaus' tale: a story of a necromancer who had enslaved a tribe of elves and stole into children's homes at night to absorb their life essence in a bid for immortality. A disgraced wizard who was rumored to conjugate with reindeer and found his power waning in recent years. Thus he set out on a quest to add to his collection of mystical artifacts to increase his magical potency. The wizard was Klaus and his ultimate goal was to challenge the mighty Titans of Grappleheim themselves, steal one of their magical belts of power and make a place for himself among the Pantheon of the Gods.

And now, his evil defeated, Klaus would do no harm and the King of Birds, his mission completed, would return to his aerie among the stars.

And what of you – the Doler of Justice? The shadow of a naked ghost? The angel of the morning? You will do as you've always done – travel the world in search of an evil worthy of your mettle, righting wrongs and serving the cause of good in your never ending quest for truth.

No fucks asked, none given.

THE END... for now.

You have made your decision. And having made it, you speak.

"It has been said that there is honor among thieves and in my travels, I have oft observed this to be truth," you begin. Then, turning to Ookla and Thaarl, "But these scoundrels are without honor of any sort. Still, I am disinclined to kill an unarmed foe and these two are far too stupid to be truly evil."

Turning your back on the thieving duo, you continue.

"I say, let us not tempt the fates, for we have more pressing matters at hand than the lives of such as these." And with that, you make a sweeping gesture, as though you were pushing the thieves out of your life as well as your mind.

To your delight, your sensitive ears detect Ookla as he pulls a throwing dirk out of his boot and takes aim. Before he has a chance to use it, you've already retrieved from your belt a star - shaped weapon you obtained on a journey to the eastern realms and launched the projectile, which plants itself directly between Ookla's eyes.

A rush of air on your left side alerts you to the fact that Ghastly Carol has removed Thaarl's nose from his face. He somehow manages to get to his feet and race to the door, but not before Ghastly Carol hurls her rapier, which finds its mark in the center of Thaarl's back. His spine severed, Thaarl slumps to the floor in an expanding pool of his own urine and tears, paralyzed.

Make haste to page 58, and let us witness the aftermath of this carnage!

29

As the daemon edges ever closer and you move nearer to your doom, you thrust one hand skyward halting the goblin in its cloven-hooved tracks.

"Halt, foul beast, and hear my enchanted voice! An exchange of rhymes shall be my battle of choice! Your leathery wings are fearsome and brutal, but I'll take you to the learning tree and make of you my pupil!" you intone with authority.

Seeing the stunned look on the daemon's face, you seize your opportunity. "Parts unknown are from whence you came. Your lust for my soul, in that I cannot place blame. But between our skill sets, you'll find quite a gulf; you are naught but a goblin – I'm the mighty Scissorwulf!"

With that, you cast your sword upon the ground and cross your arms across your chest, which puffs out like that of a peacock! No doubt you have beaten this rhyming daemon at its own game.

And mayhap you would have, if indeed such a creature it were. But the beast spoke true when it admitted it only dabbled in cadence. While you struggled to do battle with verse, the razor sharp blades of its mind found a home within your psyche. The daemon took advantage of your arrogance and assumed full control of your body at that moment, forcing your own will into a cage of psychic energy it constructed within your own human mind.

This had all been part of its plan – the manipulation of treasure hunters and thieves to obtain objects bearing magical power, such as the fabled unicorn horn. The use of said power to mystify a being of strength such as yourself and finally, domination of a corporeal form. You remain quite awake and aware as the beast steals your body, and are forced to bear witness to the savagery the creature inflicts on the innocent while wearing your face. A reign of terror which continues unabated for many years to come until you are eventually burned at the stake by a group of Pilgrim daemon hunters.

And that shall be THE END of you.

Stealing a glance at Ookla and Thaarl, whose tear-stained faces and urine soaked pantaloons indicate that they're likely willing to agree with anything, you straighten your shoulders and motion toward the cowardly scallywags hiding under the table in their own excrement.

"Why yes, indeed I am. May I presume you are the one we are here to meet?"

"Presume what you will, stranger," the pirate replies, "It makes no difference to Altazzarrian steel!"

And with that, she attacks! While you were busy coming up with a plan and salivating over her ample bosom, which threaten to explode from her bodice like overripe fruit, Ghastly Carol had removed from its sheath her rapier and thrust it in a manner not unlike the thoughts which pervaded your perversions. The blade glances against your ribcage, drawing blood. It was only your battle hardened reflexes that saved you from incurring a fatal wound.

Seizing the opportunity, Ookla and Thaarl scurry from their hiding spot under the table and run toward the door, each clutching a satchel filled with the contraband that they had come here to auction.

Will they make it? And what of you? The only way to find out what happens is to turn to page 40.

"It would seem that my work here is done." You sheepishly suggest to the now virile magus. But any attempt to rescind your hand from his results in Klaus' grip tightening around yours.

You try to pull away, but the old man's clutch is impenetrable! Your strength seems to be lessening as his grows stronger. Indeed, the Widowmaker bears a weight upon your back you haven't felt since you first found her, when nary a whisker wove its way upon your chin. Would an attack now even be possible?

Finally, Klaus releases his grip as you slump to the floor of the sleigh, weakened to the point of sheer exhaustion. Casting a glance at your body, you find yourself but a shell of your former glory. Where once muscle and sinew layered upon each other to create brawny thews, there was but skin and bone left. What was once a virile praetorian appeared now as naught but a wizened old man, edging ever closer to death's sweet embrace.

Klaus, on the other hand, removes his splendid robes to reveal a muscled, sinewy body like carved granite. His throbbing erection stands before you like the proud ornamentation of a ship's bow.

"The power is mine once more!" Klaus cries, still holding the gleaming unicorn antler aloft. His other hand moves toward his member, aiming it at you like a scepter. You are too weak to prevent his fervent stroking, which quickly results in a climax so powerful, he emits a beam of glowing light from his shaft which bathes your entire body, burning away flesh from bone and leaving nothing behind but a pile of soot and cartilage to be swept away by the blustery wind.

THE END.

"Fuck this shit" you say, returning the deadliest of weapons to her place of rest. Spinning on your heel, you commence with the making of the haste, fully intending to exit the premises as swiftly as possible. You've born witness to a great many things in your time and typically, when a magical object begins to glow, it's time to get to steppin'.

But it is for naught. For when a magical item is activated and it's power becomes known to the world, notice is given to any and all creatures sensitive to such things. And in a nearby cave just outside of town, hidden from the prying eyes of mortals, there was a stirring in the darkness. For this cave was filled with Care-a-dactyls, kin to the unicorn and the manticore and magical creatures in the highest order. Awakened, these enormous, brightly colored beasts spread their leathery wings and took to the air with only love on their small, primitive minds. Love, and the clarion call of the once lost horn of the horny horse.

Within seconds, you find yourself surrounded. The Care-a-dactyls snatched up the unicorn horns and with them, you! Seeking only love and the making of it, the creatures embraced you in their talons, trading you back and forth between them, blissfully unaware that their games of passion were tearing you to pieces. Weakened, you are unable to fight as they carry you back to their cave.

Once there, the beasts add the unicorn horns, as well as the enchanted blade of the Widowmaker to their treasure trove of magical items. Placing you in their nest of love, the Care-a-dactyls do with you what they were born to do. They commence with copulation, both with each other and with you, a horror so vile, your mind goes blank, unable to comprehend it. Thankfully, you die quickly and this is...

THE END.

Weighing your options and taking note of the bloodshed you have born witness to today, you realize that it may be better to simply bid the old man a fond farewell and make your way in the world on your own. While such actions are unlikely to curry favor with Mother Nature and the souls of the unicorns who lost both their lives and their antlers will never know justice, but it was a much wiser man than you who once opined "He who fights and runs away lives to fight another day." Cowardice may not be in your nature, but tangling with a wizard is folly.

"I'm sorry sir, but I must be on my way," you tell the old man, "For I am but a simple traveller caught up in a tale that is not mine to tell and I am clearly in over my head."

Casting his eyes toward the floor and shaking his head, the old man replies, "Well, I'm sorry to hear that, son. And even sorrier to have to use what little bit of energy I've got left for this."

When the old man raises his eyes to meet yours, you notice they are glowing green. It will be the last thing you ever see.

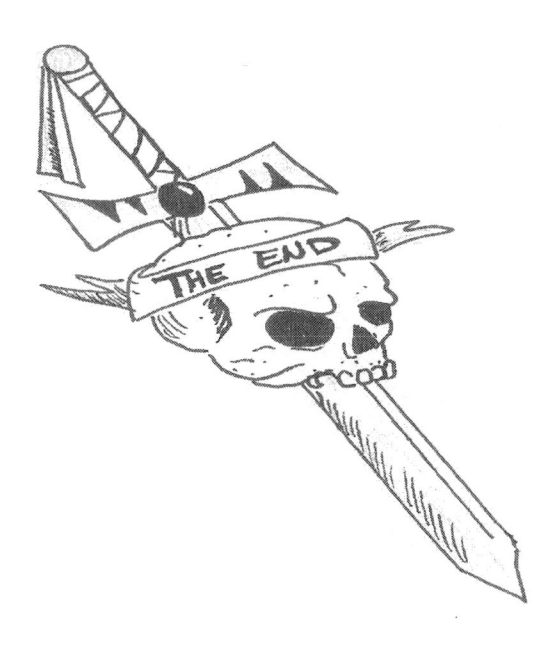

Despite the pouring rain, the crashing sea, the skittering and chittering of the mermonkeys, the bellowing of the Cocktopus and various other shouts, screams and sounds of melee, you are able to pinpoint Ghastly Carol's exact location by the sound of her screams. A scream which you knew all to well, as one quite similar came from your own lungs mere moments ago – it is the sound of one who is being eaten alive by mermonkys.

You turn on your heel, eager to make your way toward your lady love, but the deck of the Lady Fingerle's Revenge is slippery and while Ghastly Carol may be a child of the water, you are not. Falling ass over teakettle, you find yourself flat on your back and besieged by mermonkeys.

Your toes and genitals already devoured, the wee beasties go for your fingers, nose and ears. Within the passing of mere seconds, the creatures have left you utterly helpless. You welcome death's ebony embrace and are thankful for two things: firstly, that the Cocktopus has torn the ship asunder and it shan't be long before all is over, and secondly, that you'll never know the horror of Ghastly Carol's fate, as the mermonkeys have already eaten your ears and eyeballs.

THE END.

Your eyes flicker open and you find yourself staring at a cold, grey ceiling. Your body is immobile and your vision is obscured by strange symbols which seem to float in the air, remaining constantly on the left side of your field of vision. They change and scroll before your eyes as you scan the room.

And what a strange room you have awoken in! The walls are covered with blinking lights and a strange sort of glass which is covered by the same scrolling and ever changing symbols dancing before your eyes. It seems to be some sort of language, but it bears no resemblance to any parlance you are familiar with.

The numbness in your body begins to fade and you realize you are strapped to a cold, metal table. You attempt to rise, to break free from your shackles, but it is no use – your body does not listen to the commands you are attempting to give it.

Suddenly, the table you are on begins to shift and elevate until you are in a standing position. The shackles release and you have control of your body again! Noticing an open door on the far side of the room, you see an avenue for escape.

If you choose to take it, turn to page 91.

If you think it's better to stay put and explore your immediate surroundings, turn to page 111.

"Let's do this!" you exclaim, settling yourself in. The red and swollen eyes of your compatriots are a clear indication that the magic of the unicorn's antler (among other illicit substances) has had a strong effect on them and it is one that you wish to enjoy as well.

Never one to back down from a challenge or new experience, you are the Scissorwulf – seeker of knowledge and traveller of uncharted lands. Your mind is an open book and each new day is a blank page, waiting for you to write on it. And today's page begins a bold new chapter which may very well be titled "That time I crushed up a unicorn horn and snorted it with a couple of talking reindeer."

And holy fuck, was it awesome. And even you, who has partaken in the sacred herbs in the hidden caves of the Seers of Anon and suckled at the teat of a goddess, have never imbibed a taste so sweet and so intoxicating. It was as though the very fabric of space and time were torn and rewoven with a needle threaded through your own mind's eye. The camaraderie and kinship you felt with these two talking reindeer was the sort of bond that can only be forged through blood or combat. Though you sat on simple logs 'round a campfire nestled in the heart of the wood, no palace could have matched its finery.

The evening wore on and your mind swirled and swam with enchantment, but there was one pressing question that would not abate – the telling of the tale of whence these two came and how they got hooked up with Klaus anyway. But perhaps it is a subject better left to rest?

Do you dare? Shall you ask? Turn to page 71 and hope no one takes offense.

Nay. You think it is best to let sleeping dogs lie and not mention something that may very well be a bit of a sore spot. Turn then to page 76 and let the revelry continue!

With the able bodied crew of the Lady Fingerle's Revenge fighting tooth and nail against the swarming threat of mermonkeys, you instead opt to take on the larger threat. A glance from Ghastly Carol suggests she'll do the same. Just then, a second tentacle smashes upon the deck, landing not one foot from where you stand! You know not what lies on the other end of that enormous tactile member which fondles the ship, but you're determined that it is high time this beast felt the caress of steel.

From a time before time, she sang to you; the Widowmaker, an ancient blade forged in the fires of antiquity. Bearing the vexation of an aggrieved witch and the sanctification of an ancient sect of magi, she has been more loyal than a trusted canine and seven times as deadly. Tonight, you work in tandem with Ghastly Carol and the unnamed, yet no less deadly (though probably neither cursed nor blessed) rapier she wields like an extension of her own soul. Not since the horsemen of legend have four worked together to cause so much destruction.

Because there's you and Carol and then your two swords. That's how we came to four. In case that was confusing.

Like a team of lumberjacks, you chop and hack at the tentacle, doing far less damage than even the weakest woodchopper ever brought upon any redwood. The beast seems nigh invulnerable! A sudden shifting of the seas and a hideous bellowing alerts you to the true extent of the danger which you face.

But to find that out, you'll have to turn to page 89!

38

The rustling grows ever louder and is soon accompanied by growling and snorting, like a deadly chorus of death. You realize that whatever is creating such a noise is surrounding you, just as the night surrounds and enfolds you in her aphotic snuggle.

The growling of the wood is matched by the growling of your stomach and you are reminded that you haven't had a bite to eat all day and are growing ever weaker with hunger. It's the middle of the night and you're standing on a killing ground that has clearly drawn scavengers from miles away. In all likelihood, you are totally and utterly fucked right now.

Shall you make a break for it and try to escape anyway? There's no shame in running. Running all the way to page 69.

Or will you make your final stand, sword in hand, like the goddamn warrior you are? Turn to page 86.

39

You've fought many a battle in your day, but ne'er with one who didn't deserve it and ne'er for the simple thrill of bloodshed. Having no enemy or benefactor in this conflict, you choose to make a hasty exit, leaving these no doubt skilled warriors to fall upon sword and spear as they will.

A friend of nature and brother to many a woodland creature, you opt to call upon one of your brethren to aid you in your flight. Inserting two fingers into your mouth, you blow, emitting an ear piercing whistle that echoes past river and dale and indeed, over the mountains themselves. An ancient song known by few, save those old enough to remember or wise enough to listen.

Without warning, save for the shrill whistle which brought them here, they appear upon the horizon. Silhouetted against the sun, their shiny chrome plumage reflects the morning star's light – for these are no ordinary eagles! Large enough to bear several men upon their robust shoulders and conceived of pinion and ingot, these magnificent birds with plume and crest of steel come screaming for vengeance and hellbent for leather from the vaults of the heavens themselves!

Sweeping low over the battlefield, the lead eagle allows you to leap upon its back as it raises you up on its wings and bears you on the breath of dawn. But unbeknownst to you, there is a cave just past the Mountains of Mayhem, in which is the resting place of a slumbering dragon that sleeps atop a mountain of gold in a deep and dark cavern. Awakened by your whistle, the dragon has become enraged and takes to the sky with naught but destruction on its mind! Mighty as those alloy eagles may be, they are still no match for a dragon and the great worm overtakes the bird and you with it. You shall make a fine dinner.

Sadly, this is THE END.

In one fluid motion, the pirate known as Count Dante's Daughter turns and launches her cutlass in the direction of the thieves. It both enters and exits Ookla's neck, sending him to the floor, gasping for air for several excruciating seconds before dying. It takes but a moment for Ghastly Carol to retrieve a whip from her belt and with a resounding *CRACK!* - Thaarl finds himself missing an ear. His hand reflexively shoots to the side of his head as the whip recoils – *CRACK*! The strap wraps 'round his wrist and he is pulled to the floor, where his nose meets the hardwood and cartilage meets brain tissue. Leaving you to tend to your wounds, Ghastly Carol crouches by the fallen hooligans and retrieves the satchels flush with contraband.

You see an opportunity arise. Carol's faith in her own abilities and the momentary distraction of dealing with Ookla and Thaarl has left her exposed. Ordinarily, you'd never stab an enemy in the back, either figuratively or literally, but given the nature of this situation, it could be your only chance at survival. Whatever shall you do?

If you bring the Widowmaker's unique brand of bloody justice down upon Ghastly Carol's person, turn now to page 19.

If you try to find another way, get thine self to page 46 posthaste!

Ignoring the now constant creaking and popping noises directly outside the walls, you focus on the task at hand and hope that Ghastly Carol hasn't noticed. But a pirate is nothing if not in tune with her ship and Carol is already half dressed before you have the opportunity to blurt out your request.

"Wait, it's probably nothing!" you plead in your gentlest voice. "Come now, fair lady, let us resume with the –"

But before you can finish your petition, a flicker of Ghastly Carol's sword has left you with one less appendage.

"Never put your pleasure before me or the safety of my ship and her crew," Carol commands, "Now GOOD DAY to you, sir!"

And with that, she is gone, like a rainbow in the dark, leaving you a bloody, whimpering, penis-less mess. Dropping to your knees, you begin to search for your fallen member, but the shock of the event and the loss of blood causes you to black out as the sounds of battle rage on the ship's deck above you.

What was the real story of those unicorn horns and what role did Ghastly Carol play? What's going on outside the ship? These are questions that shall remain forever unanswered and at this moment, you find yourself unable to care much anyway. Soon, you shall slip beyond the veil and fall into unconsciousness and enter the eternal void of darkness.

For you, selfish fool, this is truly ...

The End.

Rising to your full height, you easily snap the flimsy bamboo snare draped over your person. A quick headcount reveals no less than seven attackers standing before you poised to kill, and no doubt an equal number behind. You smile, for the Scissorwulf is a man who drinks deep of the cup of life and the Widowmaker is a blade with an undying thirst for evil blood. And a challenge is always welcome.

Reaching over your shoulder, you whisper a hushed oath. There are a great many gods in the cosmos, and none to which you profess fealty, but tonight's battle will be dedicated to The Machomian, a savage god and ruler of a Kingdom of Madness. It is said that The Machomian guides the elbows of warriors as they swing their swords on the battlefields and instills in them a berserker rage. Tonight, against odds such as these, you shall need all the help you can get; be it mortal, divine or the heavenly steel of the Widowmaker, lying in wait in her scabbard on your back, ready to sing a deadly duet of violence with the only crooner who can harmonize with her dulcet tones.

But the Widowmaker is gone! The drug tipped dart which poisoned you must've been stronger than you thought and this group of ne'er do wells has pilfered your sword in the confusion!

Your mind muddled and senses dulled, you realize that this is a unique poison – one you have never encountered and far too powerful for even your hearty constitution. Your body begins to give out on you and you drop to your knees before finally coming to rest upon the cold wetness of the forest floor. The world spins as though you are intoxicated and soon, everything is black.

Turn now to page 12.

Taking stock of your surroundings, you find yourself standing on a mountainside, your body whole again. Beneath you, far below the treacherous precipice upon which you stand, is a pit of fiery magma and bathing in it are deadly lava dogs – ravenous canines of pure basalt and slag, their hides can withstand any heat and their teeth can pierce even rock. The stench of brimstone pervades the air, which seems to pulse and breathe with living flame.

Though you are naked as the day you were born, in your right hand is the Widowmaker, the most powerful weapon you have ever encountered. Long has she guarded you from the foe and led you in ways everlasting, protecting you from death and keeping you from harm. A companion more trustworthy than any brother who has stood with you in the heat of battle or any lover who has lain in the heat of the boudoir. Your genitals, which had heretofore been receding inside of your body cavity due to fear, now venture forth to their former flaccidity, secure in the knowledge that victory would be yours today.

And then you see the daemon. Standing ten feet tall with a chest not unlike the aged barrels of rye ol' Bigjaw McGraw used to serve at the watering hole back home before his untimely death at the hands of an enraged steer, the daemon's cloven hooves dig into the dirt as its low grumble turns into laughter. With flesh is as charred as the scorched and barren earth upon which it stands, the creature's enormous head bears the weight of a set of massive antlers. Betwixt it's thighs, the goblin possesses the loins of both sexes – engorged with lust and a desire to see blood shed. It's mouth is a sickening mess of teeth as sharp as daggers and two forked tongues spit out a variety of curses and taunts, along with actual spit, which is totally grody.

We gonna do this? Turn to page 124.

Mayhap thou canst find a way to trick this foul creature? Turneth thine page to eighty and eight.

Your hand instinctively covers your face, both as an attempt to shield your eyes from the bewildering light emanating from the figure which was once Thaarl and to protect yourself from the cosmic figure who stands exposed before you – a being of pure, brilliant radiance. Your mind reels at what is happening and what is yet to come. What is this creature masquerading as a common thief and what are its intentions? Did you seal your fate when you attempted to slay it? Finally, the creature speaks in a voice that resounds through your earholes and into your soul, echoing throughout eternity.

"Your thirst for blood shall be your undoing, mortal fool! For on this day, it is no common hooligan whose life you have attempted to extinguish, but the undying flame of a titan – and that choice shall be your doooooooom!"

And he totally stretches out the "doooooom" just like that, to really hammer it home.

You find yourself unable to move as this illuminated being moves toward you. His/her/its form begins to change before your eyes. It is at once human and completely alien. It's legs twist and turn into tentacles and in the blink of your mind's eye, you see before you a woman with the head of a bird, as naked as the day she was born – her belly swollen with child. She becomes a centaur, then a wolf walking upright and wearing a tie as though it were a man. Finally, as this strange being touches you upon your brow with its outstretched hand, you look upon the face of your father – your true father, before darkness envelops you: a darkness so total and all-encompassing, you lose all sense of being. Your form and shape are unknown to you. Sound and vision no longer exist, if indeed they ever did.

And soon, you are one with the darkness. As you always were; as you always shall be.

This is THE END, beautiful friend.

"Fuck this shit" you say quietly, recognizing the sad state of affairs you've found yourself in. Devoid of clothing, hope or any idea what in blue blazes is even going on with all of this unicorn business (save for the incredible buzz and raging erection which still lingered as a result of the inhaling of said refreshment), you've recognized that the inevitable has happened and it's time to abandon ship. Clearly, life is pissed at you and yours.

Spying Ghastly Carol on the far side of the deck, you make haste. Using the ship's rigging, you swing toward her, over the head of the swarming mermonkeys, and snatch her up in your arms, finally landing in a dinghy, ready to make your escape.

"Unhand me!" Ghastly Carol shouts as the escape craft hits the water. "Retreat is the path of the coward! I shan't be a party to it!"

But then another terrifying crash alerts you to the fact that the Cocktopus has torn the Lady Fingerle's Revenge asunder and the entirety of the crew has been dragged down to a watery grave by those vile little mermonkeys. Surely, all is fucked.

"I shall avenge my crew!" Carol shouts, leaping from the dinghy and landing atop the Cocktopus' enormous head, planting her sword in its right eye.

All may be lost, but you have an opportunity to die with pride, as a Doler of Justice, if you but turn to page 99.

Naw, that bitch is crazy. Turn to page 121.

46

You're not stupid – you know better than to attack an Altazzarrian pirate, even one whose back is turned. You'll just have to find another way out of this situation. Lucky for you, someone else has born witness to your plight.

You hadn't noticed the wizened old man sitting in the corner for the past hour, most likely because you've been too busy fighting for your life. But he had most definitely taken notice of you. Clad in beggar's rags, the elderly gent quietly sipped on an elderberry juice while observing the events which unfolded before him. Until now...

Rising from his wooden chair, the old man places his right hand on the amulet he wears about his neck while the left is thrust under the waistband of his tattered pants. Vigorously stroking with both hands, the old man quietly recites an incantation in some long-forgotten tongue. The amulet becomes illuminated with a fiery green blaze while the crotchital area of his pants gives rise to a magic wand of a different sort. The air becomes hazy and strange symbols appear around the old man. For a moment, he appears bearded and robust, as vigorous as a young hero in his prime.

Then – a blinding flash of green light! And all the world goes dark.

Until you turn to page 49.

"Well, this is my stop!" you shout to Klaus as you prepare to launch yourself out of the mobile death trap that his broken down old cart has become. "Shine on, you crazy diamond!"

And with that, you leap out of his rambling, ramshackle old cart. You can't be sure, but you think you hear him cry out and reach for you as you fall. But at the speed he's going, he's far and away before his mouth forms even the first syllable.

Perhaps you misjudged the briskness of the cart's dispatch or even your own abilities (if indeed such a mistake is possible), or perhaps the ground in these woods is a bit harder than you're accustomed to – at any rate, you don't quite land on your feet. You instinctively tuck and roll with the fall, for all the good it does.

Is it the snapping of twigs and the crackling of dry autumn leaves beneath you? Or is it the myriad of tiny bones within your hands that shatter as your body continues its revolution? By the time you come to a stop, your form is naught but a bloody bag of bones and your field of vision is obscured by a crimson mask.

Ironically, the very birds you wished to escape from return to find your immobile carcass lying still – but still quite alive – lying in the forest glen. Their incessant cawing sounds are akin to laughter as they pluck at your eyes, nibble on your ears and feast upon your flesh.

You beg whatever god will listen to your cries that it will soon be over. That you shall quickly reach...

THE END.

48

A frantic feeling begins to overtake your mind, which is understandable, as you are possessed by a daemon. This particular daemon continues to speak in a calm and rational voice as it bedazzles you with a barrage of strange symbols and flashing lights.

[DANGER! DISASTER IMMINENT! DANGER! DISASTER IMMINENT!]

The words mean nothing to you, but they continue unabated for several moments as you tear the small room apart in your search for iron – the one metal every daemon fears. No magus yourself, your skills and knowledge in the whys and wherefores of necromancy are near nil, but one of the earliest lessons learned by those who choose to walk the warrior's path is that iron is the natural enemy of those born in the fiery realms of chaos and parts unknown.

As you smash the walls and shelves of your tiny prison, it begins to feel as though the very ground you trod upon is about to be rent asunder.

The messages continue...

[DANGER! QUAKE DETECTED! DANGER IMMINENT!]

Being unfamiliar with this strange tongue, and accepting it as the trickery of a goblin, you ignore the warnings and continue on your search. A barbarian warrior from millennia gone by, how could you know what an earthquake is, or that the computer implanted in your cyborg brain by whomever discovered your near dead body whilst on a routine mission in their time machine and brought you to their post-apocalyptic present to rebuild you as a half man half technological marvel was warning you of a threat? The words were as foreign as the invading force which had destroyed this world in a nuclear holocaust so long ago. The sound and vision and no meaning until the walls tumbled down upon you and the earth fell to pieces under your feet.

One final incomprehensible message flashed before your eyes...

[SYSTEM OVERRIDE – RESERVE POWER DEPLETED]

And then all was black. Forevermore.

Unsure of how long you've been asleep, you awaken inside the Regal Beagle next to what you can only assume are the remains of Ookla, Thaarl and Ghastly Carol. It amount to little more than a pile of smoldering bones, the flesh and clothing completely seared away. Looking around, it would seem that the events of the day had never occurred. Scanning the tavern, you spot the old man cleaning the last spots of blood from the table where you had been sitting. He may be a wicked purveyor of black magic and death, but at least the old man was tidy.

"Feeling better, old chap?" he inquires upon noticing your wakefulness.

"I feel as though a turbobeest has trampled my skull." You reply. Stealing a glance at the still smoking pile of bones around you, you inquire why the old man had let you live.

"Well, son... I have my tricks, but I'm still an old man. I've got a long journey before me and I could use a man like you – someone who's handy with the steel, if you catch my meaning. What do you say, paladin? Are you game for some adventure? There's plenty of loot in it for you!"

A quest! Suspicious as the old man is, such an adventure could prove fruitful for one who seeks to avenge the slaying of the sacred and long lost unicorn. Join him on page 59.

Or maybe you should just bid him adieu and go about your merry way? You have better things to do than tangle with a warlock – especially one who fondles himself whilst performing magic. Your path lies on page 33.

The once proud city of Gran'daven is now only a haven for evil. Known for it's crooked citizens, crooked public officials and crooked streets; it is also known for having a particularly efficient waste system, which was often used as a means of getting in and out of the city unnoticed, as well as an effective method of disposing of bodies. As such, it seems likely that the thief who snatched the satchel brimming with the horny horse's horns would use the sewers as an escape route.

Armed only with this knowledge and The Widowmaker slung about your back, you remove a manhole cover, jump inside and begin your hunt in the dimly lit channel. Trudging through ankle deep sludge infested with rats, snakes and all manner of insect, you follow the slight current and make your way east, toward the Remulite River. You must make haste, for if the burglar reaches the river, they will no doubt use one of its many tributaries to go wherever their heart desires and be lost to you forever.

Doing your best to avoid making too much noise, you make your way through the murky darkness for several minutes before reaching a fork in the tunnel! You have but two choices and you'd better decide quickly!

To follow the left hand path, turn to page 97.

If you choose to go right, turn then to page 119.

Gripping the unicorn's horn in one hand, Klaus offers you the other. Knowing full well where that hand has been but seeing no reasonable alternative, you take his sweaty, calloused palm in your left hand, struggling to maintain control of the caribou with the reins in your right.

The old wizard again begins to recite an ancient incantation in a strange, forgotten language. Or maybe it's not really all that ancient? Admittedly, you know little of incantations, so it could very well be one of the modern variety, written by some travelling necromancer just last week. It's not like you'd know the difference.

Anyhoo, as the words pass between Klaus' chapped lips, a change begins to overtake him. The unicorn's horn becomes illuminated as the chanting grows louder. Soon, the light encompasses the entire cart. Klaus' weathered visage seems to shimmer, then shift – his wiry frame begins to fill out and his face becomes that of a younger man before your very eyes. But the metamorphosis isn't limited to the old wizard; looking about you, two realities flicker in and out of existence – one in which the cart and its owner are battered and worn, as you know them, and another in which both are lustrous and splendorous, the cart bedecked with gold, satin and jewels while the old man takes on the appearance of a jolly and plump old elf.

So transfixed are you on the glamour, you scarcely realize that you are flying.

What the deuce? Turn to page 82 for an explanation!

A warrior born and a warrior bred, sooner or later you'll be a warrior dead. And if indeed it must be this day that the grim specter of death finally finds you, let it be with a blade in your hand and the blood of your enemies spilled upon the rippling muscles of your heaving chest.

As you turn, your right hand instinctively reaches for The Widowmaker as it has so many times past. Time slows down and everything turns red as you flip the switch inside your mind and ready yourself for the bloodbath that is to ensue. You say a silent prayer to The Machomian – of all the gods, it is the savage king who sits upon the throne of the Kingdom of Madness who deserves the honor of this day. And then, you come face to face with an abomination so vile, so unspeakable, so repugnant, that it redefines each of those words for you henceforth.

The behemoth stares back at you with dozens of eyes perched atop a bulging, misshapen cranium, its girth threatening to fill the entire doorframe. Its jaws are filled with hundreds of jagged teeth dripping with blood and mucous. The beast's bloated body is barely supported by thin, spidery legs and a handful of slime covered tentacles. Whatever this thing is, you can only assume that its been lurking in these labyrinthine catacombs for many years, feasting upon hobos and wayward criminals who sought refuge and escape in these tunnels – some of whom can actually be seen within the creature's belly, which surged with bioluminescence when the beast breathed. In the monster's transparent abdomen, you can just barely make out the skeletal remains of several mangled human forms as well as... unicorn horns!

It will be a pleasure to split this beast open from crotch to crown, if you but turn to page 127.

Now you are surrounded. 16 deadly hooves initiate what sages and seers of ancient times referred to as "the Deadly Prance" – a ritual dance intended to distract the prey of a pack of weredeer. A sort of hypnosis, the Deadly Prance lulls the victim into a half sleep, leaving them open to a killing blow.

But you are not some hapless rabbit, living life at the whims of the great horned owl! Nay, you are the proud and mighty Scissorwulf, slayer of dragons and imbiber of many a sacred herb. Yours is to kill, not to be killed! And while you know that death will someday envelop you in her warm embrace, today shall not be that day!

Today it is you who shall mount the offensive, not these frail beasts! You fake left then lunge right, letting The Widowmaker lead you as her old steel is thrust into the throat of the closest weredeer. Realizing that another is mounting its attack from the rear, you turn and in a graceful spinning motion, relieve the aggressor's shoulders of the burden of carrying his head.

Only two remain. Surely this is your final hour. Or minute... whatever.

Shall you stand your ground and fight on page 92?

What choice do you have? Turn to page 92 anyway!

You race back to the street, the voice in your head continuing to mock you, growing increasingly louder yet maintaining its cool, non-emotional tone while more indecipherable confabulations danced before your eyes.

[DANGER! WARNING! THREAT IMMINENT! DANGER!]

Your mind reels, but a cursory glance around your immediate vicinity reveals a wrought iron fence surrounding what's left of a nearby building. No doubt it was crafted in an earlier time to keep out rogues and scoundrels. All for naught, as its inhabitants perished anyway in whatever plague decimated this barren wasteland.

With a running leap, you hurl your body onto the spiked railing, briefly considering the possibility that the daemon inhabiting your mind and body has created an illusion so full that nothing – not even this fence – can be accepted as real. You may very well be jumping into a cool and refreshing body of water!

The watery crunch you hear as you land upon the row of iron prongs assures you that the fence is indeed quite real, the pain that follows serving as a perverse punctuation mark. Your eyes pinch shut as you attempt not to block the pain, but to accept it as a natural part of being and thereby conquer it, as you were taught so long ago in the courtyards of the monasteries of the Ma'twelzian monks. And when you open them again, the whole world has turned to fire.

Continue to page 43.

"Fuck this shit." You reply and turn to leave. For you are the shadow witnessed in the dead of night, you are your own spirit animal and the master of a destiny which you and you alone create. Nary a fuck have you requested in your lifetime, and nary a fuck hath you given.

"Fare thee well, oh Scisorwolf," the King of Birds calls out to you as you walk away. Of course, he knows you – he has eyes and ears as far as a bird can fly. He knew the answer to your question before he even asked.

"I know your soul as well," he continues, "Worry not about your quest, for it ended with the death of Klaus, an old man who, grieving the loss of his wife and children, turned to sorcery and the manufacture of fine toys and playthings. His desire to restore his family to life was what led him to seek out the purest form of magic that has ever graced this earth – the unicorn's horn. But his grief drove him mad and upon gaining such magic turned his soul black and evil. It is said that power corrupts, and absolute power corrupts absolutely. Klaus wished to reign supreme among necromancers and wreak havoc upon the world as a form of revenge upon life itself. But thanks to you, I was able to shift the balance of power back to the light."

You turn to face him, but the King of Birds is nowhere to be found. In his place is a fluttering of feathers and the rustling of leaves in the wind. This adventure is over, but surely another is yet to begin.

A powerful man with powerful tastes, your thirst for knowledge is as great as your thirst for vengeance. The lone antler of the horny horse has already been ground into powder – to allow a gift so rare to go unused would surely be a crime nearly as great as the slaying of such a fine beast. And the odds of this opportunity presenting itself again are nil. You need to snort that shit.

Bringing the bowel to your face, you bury your nostrils in the dust which coats the bottom. Inhaling deeply, the powder fills your nostrils and travels deep within your sinus cavities, infusing itself with your very soul.

Reality slips away, replaced by an intrinsic authenticity as mendacious as a lark and as honest as a newborn calf. The magicks of the unicorn's horn work their eldritch charms upon your mind and past, present and future mingle in a bitches brew of arcane flavors seasoned with mystic delights.

A life passes before your eyes – is it your own? Individual memories take on a solid form as the world around you becomes soft and gelatinous. You feel yourself sinking, bogged down by the weight of those memories.

Turn to page 116 to continue on this trip.

RESISTANCE IS FUTILE!

TURN TO PAGE 80 ANYWAY!

"Let us make haste!" Ghastly Carol urges as she snatches the unicorn horn filled satchels Ookla and Thaarl had been carrying. "I wish to show you my ship and begin our adventure together in earnest!"

"I can think of naught else." You reply. And, because you're pretty sure she isn't just talking about a boat (but only like, 99% sure) you add "Unfurl your sails and let me board your frigate!" because that way, if you're not reading her correctly, you can still play it off like you're just talking about a boat and not doin' the nasty.

Leaving the carnage filled tavern, the two of you make your way to the nearby docks of Gran'daven, where Ghastly Carol leads you to a 40 cannon frigate which she presents as The Lady Fingerle's Revenge.

She was a mighty ship, crafted to transport slaves and spice from Mopeepum under the reign of Phantasia, Queen of Giles. Originally christened "the Handsome Bastard", the ship had been liberated on her maiden voyage when the slaves revolted, and lost at sea for several months. Though the slaves were able to stage a mutiny and slaughter the entire crew, they were not knowledgeable in the ways of managing a ship, as Mopeepum is a landlocked country and would have no use for such things. The people of Giles, as superstitious as they were pale and joyless, assumed the ship to be doubly haunted by the ghosts of both the crew and the slaves and never bothered to search for the lost vessel. Mayhap the priests of their corrupt religions could handle one exorcism, but a ship that was *doubly* haunted? Not worth the money or manpower. And so, the ship remained lost at sea.

Discovered and salvaged by Alkalian traders, the vessels' crew and cargo were overtaken several years later by the diabolical pirate Larry Robicheaux, also known as Plaquebeard, who lost the ship (as well as his heart) to Ghastly Carol in a game of gin rummy.

To learn more about the rich history of this and other historical ships, visit your local library. Or just turn to page 79.

You've tangled with a wizard or two in your day and you know better than to make one angry. Though you're more than a little bit leery of the prospect of travelling with this old coot, you realize that patience is likely a good virtue to have at this stage of the game. It got you this far. At best, this will lead to an opportunity to avenge the slain unicorns and at worst, you'll just have to find a way to escape when the opportunity presents itself. Besides, you had to figure there was going to be some wizard shit going on at some point, didn't you?

"Tis true that I know my way around a fight," you answer the old man, "but it seems you have your own methods, which are far more effective than fisticuffs and swordplay. Of what use could I be to you, old man?"

"I do have a trick or two up my tattered old sleeve," the ancient mage replies, "but at my age, it takes a bit more effort to wave this wand and such efforts leave me tired and worn. I need a hearty man full of vigor to aid me in times such as those. And besides, at my age, I have little use for gold. Better to share the spoils of my journey and pass along what knowledge I have to one young enough to use it."

There is logic in the old man's words and your fear of wizardry is not enough to snuff out the blaze which burns fiery hot within your heart – the flame of justice which seeks redress for the slaying of those noble and beautiful spirits, the ancient unicorns. That is the very blaze which set you on this journey in the first place!

"Alright then, old man, let us hear more about this journey of yours..."

Turn to page 64 to hear what he has to say!

60

You remember an old saying you heard once from a foot soldier in the Branch Lucridian Royal Army: "Entrap me once, shame on you. Entrap me again, and the shame of this misfortune now lies heavy upon my own shoulders." Using this less than elegant metaphor as your guide, you decide that ample shelter can be found elsewhere. All of these buildings, though no longer fit to make a permanent residence in, are still sound enough to weather the elements for a night.

Finding a nearby alleyway, you gather some scraps of lumber and craft a lean-to. You ascertain that it would be wise to remain out of doors, lest you be trapped by an attacker or have one of those ramshackle old buildings collapse on you. Sitting down and making yourself comfortable, you discover that sleep will not find you. Now that you've got some degree of safety, you reflect upon your surroundings and the events of the past few days. Hours ago, you were making love to the most beautiful pirate you'd ever laid eyes upon, then besieged by a bevy of sea creatures and left near death. And now... are you metal, are you man? What a long, strange journey this has been. And what of the daemon who possesses you? Your mind begins to reel until, having reached the end of your resolve, give voice to your fears.

"Where am I? What have I become?" you scream to the sky. A moments silence follows and then a whirring noise inside your head leads to more strange symbols dancing before your eyes. Finally, a cold emotionless voice that is not your own speaks to you from a place within your own thoughts.

"[QUERY]: LOCATION: DESIGNATE: ARCADIA, Y:87 POST-MIU"

"[QUERY]: IDENTIFICATION: DESIGNATE: AGENT SCISSORWULF PANZER CLASS CYBORG"

"ANY FURTHER QUERIES?" the voice asked.

What's all this then? Turn to page 93 to find out!

Throughout the course of your travels, you have learned a great many things. Chief among them is that you still have a great many more to learn. But one thing you do know is that under no circumstances does one fuck with a power hungry, raving mad would-be god/sorcerer who has a minimum of two enchanted relics in his possession. Since the King of Birds clearly fits that bill, you decide that it is high time to turn tail and run.

You make it about five feet before a tiny willow tit flits about your eyes, causing you to trip and tumble ass-over-teakettle onto the hard dirt. Before you know it, you are surrounded by starlings, robins and swallows. It seems that you shall suffer the same fate as poor old Klaus.

But it is not to be. Indeed, the incessant flapping of wings brings you near insanity. Indeed, your flesh is pecked away by steely beaks. But death does not come for you, no matter how much you wish it would.

With the three mystical artifacts in his possession, the King of Birds is nigh omnipotent and as such, he possesses the godlike ability to not only take life, but to give it. And so he does, allowing his bird minions to bring you to the brink of death, only to restore you to health so that they might do it again. Your mind soon shatters as your entire existence becomes one of pain and misery – a misery that seems to have begun at the dawn of time and continues forevermore.

THE END.

Ghastly Carol leaves you little choice but to join her group of buccaneers on the high seas; though in truth, you were grateful for it. Either she too was on the trail of those who would traffic in mystical artifacts and contraband relics, or it was Count Dante's Daughter herself who was responsible for such a vile act. If it were the former, you looked forward to joining this deadly corsair as she wreaked havoc upon your common foe. But if it turned out to be the latter... you held out hope that your steel was strong enough. For few cross swords with Altazzarrian pirates and live to tell the tale.

Gathering up the satchels which burst at the seams with unicorn horns, Ghastly Carol motions toward Ookla and Thaarl.

"First, there is the matter of these two knaves." Carol says, casting an angry eye at the urine soaked thieves. "It will do my reputation no good to let them live, yet they are so witless, I would feel a great guilt ending their worthless lives. What say you, oh Doler of Justice? What end seems fitting for two such as these?"

Shall you kill them? Turn to page 65 to do so.

Poor Ookla and Thaarl, let them go! Turn to page 28.

Closing one eye, you take careful stock of the thief and his path. To most observers, the thief's weaving in and out of the crowd would seem completely random, but not to your trained and watchful eye. There is an order to the path – a natural rhythm that only a master hunter such as yourself could ever recognize. Stilling your mind and controlling your breathing, you reach out with your other senses, feeling the pulse and tempo of the buildings, the people, the crowd. Slowly, you unsheathe the Widowmaker from her sheath where she hangs upon your back, waking her from her slumber. And once awoken, her thirsty steel cannot sleep until blood has been shed.

Reeling back, you heave the blade through the air, aiming not for where the thief is, but for where he is going to be. With a resounding THUNK!, you finds your mark. Retrieving your prize will be easy, due to the close proximity of the buildings in Gran'daven. In a matter of seconds, you close the distance between you and your prey and leap to the street below.

Not wishing to be caught up in any trouble, the crowd has already dispersed, leaving the street empty. As you clean the blood from your blade, you notice that in the throes of death, the thief dropped the bag full of unicorn horns, which have scattered throughout the street. Curiously, they begin to glow.

You'd better gather these up before someone notices. Turn to page 85.

Fuck it – when shit starts glowing, it's usually a good time to run. Your destination lies on page 32.

The old man leads you out of the tavern, picking up the pouches left behind by Ookla and Thaarl along the way. You pause for a moment to inspect the remains of the thieves and of Ghastly Carol, a dangerous pirate, fierce warrior and cunning strategist whose legend preceded her. While your paths may have put you at odds today, you were never truly enemies. What might have been? When time allows, you will remember to imbibe a drink in her honor.

You follow the old man behind the tavern to discover a small carriage drawn not by horse, but by two large reindeer! From the looks of them, the deer have seen better days. Their fur is worn and grey and they have a tired sadness in their eyes.

"Meet Dunder and Blixem." The old man says as he strokes the necks of the creatures and feeds them some old carrots he pulls out of his pocket. "I used to have a whole team of 'em, but that was another lifetime. Now it's just the three of us left. They aren't exactly pretty and they fart a lot, but they get the job done. Now, hop into my cart and I'll tell you where we're headed."

You follow the old man's lead and take your seat. The rickety cart creaks and groans as you enter and you wonder if it will collapse under your combined weight. The old man offers you his hand.

"Don't think I caught your name, son."

"Men know me as the Scissorwulf." You reply.

"And I am Klaus." The old man says with a warm smile and a twinkle in his eye.

Turneth now to page 74.

There is truth to Ghastly Carol's words and you cannot deny it. It does a pirate no good to leave behind any survivors. They might squeal and bring retribution upon you and perhaps more importantly, allowing scalawags to walk away unharmed would do no favors for the reputation of said pirate. A warm and gentle soul has never inflicted fear into the hearts of men. Without a dangerous reputation, what is a pirate but a black flag with a skull on it? Besides, these two assholes were carrying a sack full of goddamn unicorn horns! Anyone foolish or evil enough to tamper with the balance of magic and nature deserves to die, right?

It is convenient that Ookla and Thaarl are kneeling side by side. You unsheathe the Widowmaker and bring her down upon the thieves, severing head from shoulders in one clean stroke as Ghastly Carol licks her lips with delight. Her face flushed as she noticed the slight rise in your loincloth. It seems that both of you feel a tingling in your nethers – perhaps bloodlust and libido go hand in hand for two such warriors as yourselves?

"Let us make haste," Carol prompts you, "I wish to show you my ship, so that we might set sail and begin our adventure in earnest!"

"Why wait?" you reply, "Unfurl your sails, maiden, and let me load this cargo in your vessel here and now! For what better place for us to celebrate than here, surrounded by the death and glory we hath wrought?"

There is a truth to your words, and Ghastly Carol cannot deny it.

Give in to your passions on page 106. Quickly!

You've encountered your fair share of evil wizards, vile dictators and downright evil warlords in your day and you've become skilled at recognizing depravity. And none have matched the level of depravity you bear witness to in Klaus' eyes right now.

Realizing that the old man's grip is enhanced by the magic which inhabits and envelops his being, you know that any attempt at retreat would be folly. Instead, you reach behind you and grasp the handle of the Widowmaker – forged of enchanted ore and honed to vorpal sharpness, she sings to you the ballad of the blade, waiting for you to bring in the harmonies.

Tightening your own grip on Klaus' hand, you draw him to you, close enough that you can smell the taste of reindeer dick upon his breath. Letting loose the fury of the Widomaker upon him, you clean his Klaus' head from his shoulders. Klaus' head falls from the sleigh to the ground miles below and his body is instantly reduced to dust, which scatters quickly in the breeze.

Now… what the hell are you going to do about this flying sleigh and reindeer?

Turn thee now to page 100.

"Goddamn it" you mutter under your breath as you break into a sprint back toward the path where Klaus lay bleeding. You have been known as many things, but "he who runs away from the screams of a wizened old man being torn to pieces by birds" is not, nor shall it ever be one of them.

As you approach Klaus' ravaged body, you realize that it is probably too late for him. His spine shattered, he is unable to crawl to safety. The ravens have already eaten his eyes, leaving his flesh for the swallows and chickadees. A small grouping of nuthatches and orioles pecks away at his knucklebones. Barely clinging to life, a weak cry escapes his lips.

A swarming storm of feathers congregates before you, forming a swirling mass which then takes the form of a man wearing a jaunty hat and a cloak of feathers! Standing before you was none other than the legendary King of Birds! A friend to all who call the sky their home, the King of Birds was known as "the Mad God" – the price he paid for the all-encompassing knowledge brought to him by his congregation of winged spies and informers. This is some fucked up shit right here. What choice shall you make now?

Do what you do best – fuck shit up with that big ol' sword you got there. Turn to page 95.

It can't hurt to hear the guy out. Turn to page 83.

Lowering her head to the nightstand, Ghastly Carol inhales deeply, drawing the fine white powder into her nostrils. She then invites you to do the same. As a lover of adventure, liver of life and seeker of new and bold adventures, you follow suit.

Immediately, your body begins to tingle. A feeling of euphoria overtakes you as your vision takes on a new sense of sharpness – colors become more vivid, textures become more ... texturey. And is someone on this ship playing a lute? You swear you can hear a lute off in the distance.

"Tell me, oh great hunter of justice," Ghastly Carol's husky voice sounds like a song, "In all your great adventures, have you ever plundered the pirate's cove?"

Your head is reeling. You cannot tell a lie now if you tried and of what good would it be to boast with a woman such as this, under the effects of a potion such as this? You admit that you are unfamiliar with the notion, but as the captain of the Lady Fingerle's Revenge begins to remove her eye patch, you understand what she has in mind. Reflecting on your life's travels, you are unsure if you've ever enjoyed yourself as much as you have tonight.

You are a respectful man, but you pledge fealty to no deity; no god or goddess holds your soul within their grasp. But that doesn't stop you from recognizing when a prime mover is at your side and you offer a silent prayer now to both Aristocraticles, the friend of the stallion and patron of wheelers, dealers and kiss stealers, who traverses the realms of man and god in his alligator boots, a magnificent gold and jeweled belt around his waist, granting riches to some and love to others; and to Polysemous, who is both god and goddess at once, the patron of all things of the sexy variety. Truly, both of these celestial beings are guiding you this night.

Suddenly, you hear a skittering on the side of the ship! Initially, you attribute it to the drugs, but when it happens again and the ship lurches, you realize something is up!

Do you spring from your bed to see what is the matter? Page 77.

Do you just keep workin' it, hoping its no big deal and Ghastly Carol will let you finish? Turn then to page 41.

What was the name of that wise old sage who once remarked that, in the game of life as well as games of chance, it was an astute and erudite fellow who possessed the foresight to know when to press forward and when to hold back? To know when to walk away... and when to run? Whomever it was that said that, they were right.

And you choose to run.

But few are wise enough to know the truth of the full moon and the terror it brings. What began as a rustling of leaves gives way to a thunder of hooves and the midnight charge of the Hamticore! A foul beast spoken of in hushed whispers by farming folk and hobos, the Hamticore was thought to be a fairy tale meant to scare children into doing their chores, but it was quite real and it was nearly upon you! Possessing the body of a lion and the head of a swine, the Hamticore traveled about upon nine cloven-hooved feet, with the tail of the scorpion as its weapon! Atop its head was a shining crown made of rainbows – a blessing from the princess who had loved him when he was a man. But her jealous father hired a wizard to put a curse on the young farmhand and trapped him in this hideous body, to roam the countryside, searching for truffles and prey and hoping to find a princess whose kiss will turn him mortal again.

Alas, there are many mysteries in the forest and the tales you heard while still a babe, suckling at your nursemaid's teat are now long forgotten. You remember not of the Hamticore, nor of the ways to defeat him. And tonight, you shall pay the price for your forgetfulness.

By the time the sun rises, the accursed Hamticore will have returned to his hidden cave to slumber and digest his meal, the carnage of tonight but the memory of a dream. And you shall be naught but a scattering of bones on the forest floor, soon to be picked clean by buzzards.

THE END.

Your mind alert and ready to spring like a steel trap, you begin to devise several strategies to combat whatever manner of attack might lie in wait to befall you. But while you are preoccupied with figuring out the answers, your assailant changes all of the questions.

Before you have an opportunity to react, you find yourself enraptured by a net and surrounded by several tenebrous figures. Clad in black from head to toe, save for a small slit in their masks through which their eyes are barely visible, your attackers move as quietly as a shadow and brandish all manner of bladed weapon.

A slight sting upon the back of your neck is followed by a burning sensation – you've been poisoned! But you've spent your life building up an immunity to poisons, part of the training you received at the hands of the man who raised you. An esteemed member of the Royal Guard until drink and carousing got the better of him, he took in an abandoned babe wrapped in swaddling clothes when a village full of superstitious hypocrites turned their backs.

Even slowed by poison and ensnared in a net, you are confident that your can kill this handful of raiders, but you'll have to escape your bonds first. Still, it is oft said that discretion is the better part of valor. Allowing yourself to be captured may grant you the opportunity to seek and deliver vengeance upon those who employed the thieves who stole the unicorn's horn, for surely these brigands must play a part in this tale as well?

Wilst thou free thine self from these shackles? Turn to page 42.

Or shall you let these assailants lead you to their stronghold? Turn then, to page 125.

Packing a pipe full of the dried and cured leaves Dunder and Blixem kept in a small tabernacle on their shelf, you light up and, after inhaling deeply of the sacred smoke, pose your question.

"So guys, I gotta ask," you address the two enchanted reindeer, "What the fuck was up with that Klaus guy?"

And so they tell you the tale. Unabashed and unashamed, they speak for hours of an elderly toymaker who turned to necromancy when his wife died, learning the eldritch arts in an attempt to bring back his lost love. He sought the dark knowledge that man cannot know and learned under the guidance of many a wicked magus and sorceress, trading his honesty for knowledge. The old toymaker came to know how to alter his shape and size and how to grant speech to the creatures of the earth. He even learned how to fly. But he never learned to bring the dead back to life.

In time, Klaus' successes and defeats drove him mad and he defeated and enslaved a tribe of elves. Upon finding a method through which he could steal the life essence from children and animals, Klaus sought immortality and to overthrow the gods themselves. To aid in this end, he sought out a great many mystical artifacts – a bag of holding, the wings of the fabulous Freebird and of course, the fabled antler of the unicorn.

This final piece of his puzzle was to be the coup de grace, which would grant him the power he so desperately sought. But you, the Doler of Justice and he who hides the universal secret of all time, you who walks through the valley of the shadow undaunted, YOU have defeated him and brought peace to the valley.

And for that, Dunder and Blixem thank you and pack up another bowl. For tonight is a time for partying, and the more you imbibe upon their drink and courtesy, the better looking those reindeer are getting. And Blixem has been eyeing you up all night.

THE END?

Don't start none, won't be none. That's always been your motto. And though the phrase might not exactly apply to this situation, its close enough. It may well serve you better to let the situation play out. Sooner or later, all will be revealed.

And indeed, in the midst of the punches thrown and general violence being bandied about the tavern, no one takes notice of a small figure shrouded in a black cloak creeping in through the window. No one, save you, who remain seated, observing rather than engaging in the mindless combat. And when this diminutive figure snatches up the parcel that Ookla and Thaarl had been carrying, you make haste and follow out the door.

Leaving the brawl behind you, you bolt out the tavern door to find a crowded city street full of citizens, vendors and travellers - but no thief. But you are the Scissorwulf, a trained tracker second only to The Venturian himself in the art of the hunt. Your skills and senses will not fail you in this endeavor.

Turn to page 117 to take to the rooftops in order to get the lay of the land.

The sewers are an excellent route for escape – turn to page 50 to track the thief underground!

You awaken in a field of dew-covered grass, miles from the forest encampment. You are unhurt and seemingly unwatched, but wear only the clothing you had on the right before, with the Widowmaker by your side as always. More loyal than any man you might call brother, or any woman you've known as a lover, the proud steel of a bygone era has long been your most dependable companion.

But what of the source of your vision quest? What of the storied horn of the horny horse? You check the sun to determine your location, quickly comprehend your situation and determine a course of action. You must travel westward to return from whence you came!

Rising like a quiet storm from all directions, the thundering sound of hooves and battle cries fill your ears. A realization comes over you – you've awoken in the midst of a field of battle! You observe two armies rushing toward you and both are unrecognizable to you. With no stake in this game, you must find a way out!

Do you stay to fight your way out? Turn then to page 101.

Or shall you call upon the Eagles? Turn to page 39.

You ride for several hours in silence, leaving the bustling city of Gran'daven behind for the quiet beauty of the forest. Your curiosity getting the better of you, you finally ask Klaus what his intentions are.

"Hush," he says, "Not now... for the forest has ears and you never know who is listening." Klaus gestures toward the trees and specifically, the ravens and chickadees perched upon the many branches of the multitude of trees surrounding you. You know full well that ravens aren't to be trusted, for their loyalty is easily bought and they are fluent in many tongues, and chickadees are just poseurs who will do whatever a cooler looking bird tells them to do. As powerful as Klaus is, it is clear he knows his enemies are stronger.

Just then, the very birds which Klaus had brought to your attention began to chirp and chatter. At first, it was but a whisper but the noise has increased until your eardrums were besieged with a cacophony of cawing! Casting your gaze skyward, you see a swarm of ebony wings bearing down upon you. It seems that Klaus' warning came too late and his enemies have arrived.

But they're just birds – surely they pose no threat to you? Turn to page 108.

Can reindeer outrun crows? To find out, turn to page 94.

Fuck this shit. You can just jump out of the cart and leave Klaus behind if you turn to page 13.

The mind of the Scissorwulf is akin to that of the hunter stalking its prey. But unlike the beasts of the wild, the Scissorwulf's mind is sharp and edgy, like the deadly steel he brandishes as a weapon. You are that Scissorwulf – your mind is your weapon. But then, so is the Widowmaker.

Relinquishing her beautiful deadliness from the scabbard in which she slumbers, the Widowmaker becomes an extension of your own self. And high grade steel forged in the fiery pits of Grappleheim can do what your steely sinew and muscle can not.

Plunging her blade deep within the slick walls of the chasm, you slow your fall, eventually coming to a halt. Stretching and extending you body to its full length, your toe finds dark and murky water beneath you. Though there is no light in the pit, you can sense movement. The water stirs in the darkness and slowly, you feel the slime covered tentacles of some cyclopean horror wrapping themselves around your ankles, making their way up your thighs and caressing your nether region. Their cold and clammy embrace causes your genitals to creep inside your body cavity like a shy turtle.

It is not until they've made their way around your neck and you feel the hot breath of the creature as it rises from the water beneath that you allow yourself to scream.

THE END.

Is it fear or is it respect that causes a man to bite his tongue? Mayhap it is both and mayhap that answer changes depending on any given situation? But tonight – this night – despite all that you have shared and all that you have seen together, you decide it is for the best to let a sleeping dog lie.

You have been many things in your lifetime – a warrior, a lover, a doler of justice and even a slave. And you, who are your own spirit animal, know that when one is forced to act against one's own will and finds the very fiber of their being held captive – it is not a subject that is easy to broach, nor a tale that comes easy in the telling.

So you keep your questions to yourself. For in truth, what good would it do to speak them? The quenching of one's thirst for knowledge should not come at the cost to another's peace of mind. So you continue to imbibe and enjoy the company of these two friends. What else happens in the dark of night, among consenting sentient beings, is for the three of you to know and no one else. And eventually, you drift off into slumber next to the blaze of the fire.

When you awaken, the fire is little more than smoldering ash and Dunder and Blixem are gone, leaving naught but memories, an aching soreness and a strange aftertaste. Packing your things, you make your way toward town. For you are the man they call the Scissorwulf and adventure ever awaits you. But for now, this particular adventure has come to THE END.

Disengaging, both you and Ghastly Carol instinctively reach for your swords even before you dress.

"Topside, now!" Carol commands. You marvel at the gazelle like speed of the Altazzarrian pirate – she's already dressed and out the door as you scramble behind her, naked as the day you were born.

Arriving on the ship's deck, you discover the source of the trouble by the light of the silvery moon. Climbing up the side of the ships hull and over the railing onto the deck are dozens of hideous sea born monstrosities.

Roughly three feet in length, the creatures appear to be simian in nature, but with gills just below their jawline. As the beasties vault over the ships railing, their true aquatic nature is revealed, for where their legs should have been you see the tail of a fish!

"MERMONKEYS!" Ghastly Carol's voice rings out. "They've infested the ship like unholy barnacles from Hell!"

And then that you notice the enormous tentacle wrapping around the ships bow.

Do you defend against the mermonkeys? Turn to page 107.

Are you going to start hacking away at that tentacle on page 37?

Though it pains you to watch any creature suffer, you force yourself to remember the facts of the situation, none of which call for mercy: Klaus slayed a bar full of people, some deserving, some not. He is most likely the ringleader of a black market unicorn horn ring, a crime for which there is no punishment too heinous. Plus, you've never met a wizard worth trusting.

So you turn your head and stuff your fingers in your ears, but you cannot block the screams of a man being torn to shreds by a group of peacocks and turtledoves. Minutes stretch into hours and the hours feel like weeks. You daren't make yourself known until the feast is over, but these avian avengers are being particularly thorough. You can hear their gleeful cawing long after Klaus' screaming stops.

Finally, there is naught left of the old wizard but bones and the birds fly away. Night falls and only when the gibbous moon has reached its zenith do you venture forth from your hiding place. Klaus was not your friend, but neither was he your enemy. You search his wagon to find a small shovel, then begin digging a grave in which to bury the bones – all that remains of the wizard and his steeds.

Your back is strong and your arms are sinewy and muscled; it doesn't take long to bury the bones and say a quiet prayer to a god you know doesn't give a damn. Suddenly, you hear a rustling in the bushes!

Turn to page 38 to find out what it is!

"The ship is said to be haunted," Ghastly Carol continues as the two of you take a tour of the craft. "But if it is, the spirits look upon me with favor, for I have had great luck in my travels."

"Indeed, the tales of your exploits are well known," you agree, "and your name is spoken with reverence and fear." You're trying to be extra nice, mostly because you're pretty much stuck on this ship now and you're kind of scared shitless that Ghastly Carol will kill you before dawn, but also because she's totally hot and maybe she likes you?

Firstly, you'd noticed that when you first boarded the ship, Carol had said "I invite you to come inside", and that didn't necessarily mean anything, but later on when you were maneuvering through a particularly tight corridor on your tour of the vessel, she'd remarked that the hallways weren't the only thing on the ship that was tight. Again, maybe she was talking about the lids on the pickle jars in the galley below, but you didn't think so.

And was she really just talking about fighting when she mentioned the size of your sword and her hope that you could find a suitable sheath for it when the battle was done? You couldn't be sure, but when you'd arrived at the galley and she commented that any hunger which could not be assuaged by the ship's cook could be sated in her boudoir (and yeah, she totally called it a boudoir too!), you were *pretty sure* you were picking up on some sexy subtext in her conversation.

Shall you continue the tour to the lady's sleeping quarters and whatever delights you might find there? Turn to page 87.

Then again, maybe you're reading too much into this? You don't want to embarrass yourself. Maybe it's time to head to bed on page 96.

The voice continues, explaining that the world had moved on. Centuries had passed since you had last walked the earth and a truly golden age had arisen. A world of marvels had come to pass where man and nature lived in harmony and great cities of emerald and jade stretched as far as the eye could see - until the invaders arrived. You understood little of what the voice explained, but it was clear that the more things changed, the more they stayed the same. War had erupted and another, more powerful clan had come to rape, pillage and plunder, leaving only heartache and ruin in their wake. That they were from another planet mattered little to you, having a primitive belief system and no concept of the world "planet".

And now, warring tribes of survivors struggled for supremacy in the wasteland that was left behind. You don't understand what a cyborg is, but apparently that's what you are now – your shattered body repaired with something the voice called "technology". Now you would serve your new master as a one-man killing machine. Same as it ever was.

Months go by and your own personality becomes submerged and converted by the voice in your head until you can no longer distinguish between the two. You continue to do battle with all manner of irradiated and mutated beast and machine and wage an unending war against a myriad of enemies. Time and existence no longer have any meaning and one day – how many decades has it been? Your master finally dies.

Free now, but with no purpose, you roam the deserted cities and wastelands, cataloguing this world you now call home. In time, the batteries which allow your mockery of an existence to carry on also die and with that, your consciousness ceases to exist.

And on that day, the ivory and black clad warrior maidens known as the Refyrie, blind as they may be, arrive upon their majestic winged zebras to carry your soul to the mead halls in the Gardens of Grappleheim, to sit at the Table of Warriors forevermore.

THE END.

A warrior born, you are not often given to flight. But in the dead of night, in the middle of nowhere, your instincts urge you to deny your true nature. For though you hunt and kill like the beasts of the wild, it is your human intellect which reminds you that tonight you deal not in a mortal domain, but in the realms of sorcery and those who would slay the fabled unicorn are no common foe to be taken lightly. You would do well to put distance between you and whatever is making this sound, should push come to shove.

Dropping the ceramic bowl and snatching up the leather sack holding the horns of the horned horse, you leap into the trees. Remembering your adventures in Loparr and the mighty apes which dwelled there, you use your powerful upper body to swing from branch to branch. In this manner, you are able to cover a vast distance in a short time, but the rustling of leaves which follows you carries with it a threat that you are unlikely to outpace. You must fight.

Scrambling to the uppermost branch of the tree, you survey the lay of the land. Your keen eyes have adjusted to the darkness but it is a challenge to make out anything distinct. The rustling noise seems to be coming from nearly every direction.

Suddenly, it strikes! What it is, you will never know. But it was efficient, it was stealthy and most of all, it was deadly.

This is ... THE END.

Peering over the edge of the cart, you realize that indeed, you are soaring through the clouds with land far below. The cart itself has transformed into a sumptuous sleigh seemingly carved out of a solid piece of gold, with cushioned seats made of rich Corinthian leather. Klaus' robust and vigorous form is ornamented in satin robes with fur trimming and a wreath of holly about his dome. Dunder and Blixem share in this rejuvenation, looking as hale and hearty as two reindeer in their prime, a spark of intelligence in their formerly black and soulless eyes. You realize that the reins lie limply in your hands – it is the deer who steer the ship now!

The swarm of hawks, chickens and roosters still follow you, but with Klaus' final recitation of a forgotten poem once spoken by the elders and soothsayers of a long dead tribe, they vanish in a flash of blinding light. You are safe.

Or are you? The flying sleigh has drawn to a stop, still hovering miles above the earth as the bloody remains of a thousand birds shower the ground below. Though the spell has been cast, Klaus still grips your hand in his sweaty meathook. The look of steely determination in his eye is gone, replaced by madness and lust.

Will you politely ask for your hand back and a ride home? Turn to page 31.

Fuck that. Skewer this asshole. Turn to page 66.

"What is your business here? Be you friend or foe?" you inquire of the being which stands before you in his feathered and plumed finery.

"I might ask the same of you, traveller!" the King of Birds replies in a shrill, yet commanding voice. "Be you a daemon in the guise of man? Or are you a hero – one of the warrior born?" Then, pointing to the bloodied remains of Klaus, now little more than a skeleton, "Was this man your traveling companion? Or was he your friend?"

You pause, wondering how to answer. Klaus was no friend to you; in fact, the only reason you were with him was because you suspected his motivations were sinister and you planned on killing him. And yet, you did return to help the old coot after leaving him to die at the hands of a flock of seagulls and various other bloodthirsty birds.

Naw... that dude was a dick. You're just a nice guy who doesn't like it when people suffer, even if they're creepy old wizards. Still, this can go down one of two ways.

Fuck it - you don't owe this bird guy anything. He's not even a real king. Turn to page 55 and be done with it.

Or you could just answer him. It's pretty clear he could kill you if you wanted to and the truth is likely the answer he's looking for anyway. Go to page 112.

You've got no place else to go and you've always trusted your instincts, so you walk right back into the very underground domicile you came from. Back down that flight of stairs and right back into that room filled with the strange glass and flickering symbols. Something tells you that you'll find the answers you seek inside, so you start inspecting – trying to decipher the strange language displayed on the glass. Finally, hours later, in a fit of frustration, you find yourself screaming (out loud? In your head?)

"What is this wretched place? What sort of monstrosity have I become?"

A calm, relaxed voice from somewhere within your psyche gives you an answer as more of those strange symbols flash before your eyes.

[QUERY] DESIGNATE; NEW YORK CITY, YEAR 2525
[QUERY] DESIGNATE: SISSORWOLF CYBERNETIC ORGANISM

So there you have it. You've clearly been possessed by a daemon.

As you lingered on the precipice between life and death, this incubus must have used its dark magic to revive you and return your lost limbs, but now resides within your mind, taunting you with hallucinations and trickery until you go mad and it can assume full control of your body. Typical daemon bullshit!

But you don't have to be a wizard to know how to deal with enchantments. The best way to deal with daemons and their dark arts is the cold, unflinching touch of iron. Perhaps there is some in this room?

Shall you take a look around? Turn to page 48.

No, but you're pretty sure there's some out in the street and it might be better to be out of doors right now; unless that's just more daemon trickery. Turn to page 54 to find out.

Shoveling the scattered antlers into the tattered leather sack, you glance around quickly, hoping that your actions go unnoticed. Unfortunately, they do not.

With the sound of a thunderclap, the clouds part and the heavens open. A bolt of light blasts forth from the sky. Sailing down the edge of the beam of luminescence was a creature that was perhaps not quite god, but far more than mortal. It has the basic shape of a man, if a man could be carved out of granite. Not that this guy is literally made of rock, but like... heavily muscled, okay?

Anyhoo, this being which stands before you has the basic shape of a man, save for his head, which is that of a proud and mighty stallion. He breathes smoke and his mane is ablaze like the roaring of a campfire. Atop his brow is a single gleaming golden horn. His entire being seems to shimmer, as though you were looking directly at the sun. It is hard to estimate the creature's height, but as he steps off of his rainbow bridge and stands before you in all of his glory, your eyes are at the same level as his enormous, veiny manhood. You hate to stare, yet you find that you can not look away, as the being demands your attention, as does its grotesquely majestic cockery. You are uncomfortable, to say the least, but you admit that this is very effective form of intimidation on the part of the horse-god thing.

"WHO DARES?!?" the creature speaks with a voice that reverberates to your marrow and threatens to burst your eardrums. "WHO DARES DEFILE THE SANCTITY OF THE WOOD?!?!"

You open your mouth to reply – to assure this otherworldly being that you have nothing to do with this atrocity and have every intention of getting to the bottom of it and doling out justice upon the defilers, but before the words can pass your lips, a brilliant blast of color burst forth from the being's golden horn, disintegrating you and leaving naught but a small dark stain, nearly indistinguishable from the rest of the filth of the city street.

THE END.

It's true that you are weary and the outcome of a battle is most likely predetermined at this point. But the same outcome holds true if you turn tail and run, especially in an unfamiliar wood. Is it not better then, to determine your own fate? To die on one's feet in conflict, rather than to flee? And you've never put much stock in fate anyway. Let the gods decree what they will; the Scissorwulf is in the business of creating destinies, not following them.

Unsheathing the Widowmaker from her resting place, you plant your feet and prepare for whatever awaits you. A cloud passes before the moon as your hunters slowly begin to emerge. You recognize them immediately but do not believe your eyes, for you thought the curse of the weredeer to be naught but myth and fairy tale, passed amongst superstitious women as they sit at their looms, frightening mischievous children into obedience. How many times had you heard "Mind your p's and q's lad, lest the weredeer steal ye away in dead of night?" as a young boy?

But here they are, and a whole damn herd of them, just as real as the nose on your face or the ancient, accursed steel in your hand. Surrounding you, frothing at the mouth and scraping the dirt with their front hooves, still wearing the torn remains of the clothing they had worn when still on two feet. You had trespassed in their sacred wood on the night of the full moon, and the toll was blood.

The first attack is easy to deflect. A young, unruly buck leaps at you and you catch him midair, snapping his neck. A second quietly follows and meets his end on the Widowmaker's tip. But the antlers of the remaining weredeer indicated that they had age on their side, for with age comes wisdom.

This shan't be easy. But then, it never is.

Turn to page 53.

As you make your way toward Ghastly Carol's sleeping quarters, still unsure of your host's intent, she casually questions if, during the downtime between your many adventures, you'd ever taken up gardening. For it would seem the lady had a garden that needed tending and you bore the air of a man with a green thumb. Sensing your confusion, the pirate assured you that the garden was landscaped and bore no weeds, but simply needed plowing.

Arriving at the Captain's quarters, you immediately fall into each other's arms, laboriously groping each other like spasmodic cephalopods. Any questions which may have lingered about this woman's intent were quickly answered. For it is impossible for two warriors such as yourselves to remain unaffected by the spilling of blood. Your heartbeats race in unison as though you were in battle, and the powerful stirring under your loincloth is met in kind by the lustful yearnings of Ghastly Carol's moist and sensuous loins.

Carol proves herself to be as adept at making love as she is with a sword. Her bedchamber becomes both classroom and church and though you have known many a lover in your time and consider yourself skilled in the gentle arts; your mind, body and soul are alight with a cornucopia of new experiences, each more delightful than the last.

During a brief pause in your carnal activities, Ghastly Carol produces the satchel carried by Ookla and Thaarl and removes from it a single unicorn's horn. Grinding the antler on a nearby nightstand produces a fine powder, much as the thieves had done last night. She then divides the white dust into several small lines of relatively the same size and looking you in the eye, asks a simple question...

"Do you like to party?"

Business is about to pick up. Page 68.

Though you are no wizard and have had no training in any sort of dark sorcery, you've learned a thing or two about daemons and goblins in your day. Chiefly that they curry in a strange form of dictum which the quick of wit can use to defeat them.

"If I am to die today, may I have the pleasure of knowing to which sort of daemon I owe my defeat?" Flattery will get you everywhere, especially when dealing with an archfiend.

"You may." The Goblin replies in an intrigued tone.

This wasn't going quite as smoothly as you'd hoped. You decide to take a more straightforward approach with your next question.

"Be you a rhyming daemon?"

"Though I drop rhymes and flow quite often, 'tis not my cadence which shall put you in a coffin." The creature's reply seemed telling... or did it?

Shit. This is confusing. Plus, it might be a lying daemon anyway, rendering any questions or answers moot. You've got to act fast though, because the beast grows ever closer with each passing moment.

Turn to page 26 if you think you can come up with a decent plan to defeat this thing fast enough.

Turn to page 29 to challenge the monster to a rap battle.

89

There is a loud creaking and the sound of splintering wood. You realize that the enormous tentacle that had been wrapped around the ship's bow has now rent it fully asunder. With a crash, another tentacle the size of a redwood tree slams onto the deck, narrowly avoiding you, while yet another wraps around the stern.

You've never seen an octopus before, nor the mighty squid or cuttlefish which roam the dark vastness of the oceans. You have heard tales of the Kracken and wondered if the creature which sought to tear this ship apart was of its ilk? For in all the myths and legends of yore, no mention had been made of feathers, which covered the slippery feelers currently wrapped around the Lady Fingerle's Revenge.

A spray of water strikes you, nearly sending you ass-over-teakettle, and again the ship lurches as though it might split up or capsize, or even break deep and take water. The screams of the crew are drowned out by a hideous noise, somewhere between a bellowing and a crowing sound. The light of the silver moon is nearly blocked by the enormous figure rising from the briny depths. You cast your eyes skyward and bear witness to the frightful hackles and razor sharp beak of that deadly legend known as The COCKTOPUS!

Will you continue to fight? Turn to page 14.

Or shall you try to escape by turning to page 45?

During your many travels down the path of the warrior, you've learned a great many things about a great many things. A battle with a would-be god in possession of a trifecta of mystical artifacts is not a fight you'll likely find yourself on the winning side of. But running would also result in death, so why not stand, as you always have, on your own two feet? Tis a far nobler death than the alternative.

And so it was that the battle which became known in legend as "Scissorwulf's Folly" took place. And as unlikely as victory was, it nonetheless occurred. For despite his legion of birds and the arcane objects he possessed, the King of Birds did not take into account The Widowmaker – that fabled blade forged in the fire pits of time before time, cursed by a witch and ordained by an arch-mage. It was this weapon, finer than any friend or lover, which shattered the Tabernacle of Endowment and tore the Rosary of Sorrows from the neck of the King of Birds. The very same sword which dealt the killing blow.

And so it was that The Scissorwulf ascended to godhood and found himself in the world beyond Parts Unknown, seated among the titans in the Gardens of Grappleheim. All that remains now are the faces and the names of those who were there when it happened, and passed the stories on to their children, and their children's children. And those stories were one day collected by a master storyteller in a fine document, which you hold in your hands right now.

THE END.

91

Without a moment's hesitation, you bolt from your position and race out the door, finding yourself in a long grey corridor devoid of windows or decoration. You keep your head on a swivel and can't seem to discern an advantage to going in any particular direction – yet, when you turn left, those incomprehensible symbols seem more positive, as if this is the correct path. Whatever this strange language is, it would seem that you are deciphering it like a champ!

So left you go, up several sets of stairs and just as you begin to question how it is that you can even move, considering the fact that you were lacking in both extremities and genitalia not so long ago, you come to a door. Could it be the way out? Racing at full speed, you raise your hands just a moment before you reach the door and realize that they are not your own! No longer flesh and blood, your limbs have become some steel, of some sort – but steel that is as pliable as cloth and mimics human movement! What manner of sorcery is this?

Bursting through the door, you tear it off of its hinges! You seem to possess a strength you have heretofore never exhibited. Passing through the doorway, you enter into the daylight of a strange new world... or what's left of one. Whatever kingdom once existed here, it must have been fantastic. But now it is but a ruin of near demolished buildings reaching toward the skies. The empty streets are in a state of disrepair and littered with trash and corpses. Roving packs of feral dogs wander here and there, looking for a meal.

Suddenly, your vision turns as red as blood and those strange symbols begin to flash erratically, as if warning you of some imminent danger. What in blazes is happening?

Turn to page 114 to get to the bottom of this craziness!

At this point, you're feeling pretty confident. You just took out four weredeer with relative ease, watching them revert to human form mere moments after you stopped their cursed hearts from beating. Was that a look of sadness in their eyes when they died, or was it gratitude? You presume it to be the latter, for the curse of the shapeshifter is ne'er one that is enjoyed.

You'll have time to reflect on that later. Right now, you've got two more demon deer ready to pounce. Rather than wait to be attacked, you mount the offensive, hurling your sword at the nearest weredeer, sending it directly through the center of its face with a sickening crunch, splintering bone and splattering bits of brain and blood on the nearby trees.

But your attack has given the final creature a moment to strike! It charges you, impaling your kidneys with its deadly sharp rack of antlers. The deer quickly backs off as you drop to your knees. The change is already upon you, for a poke in the kidneys from the enchanted rack of a weredeer is the method by which the curse is passed on.

A silent chorus reverberates in your ears. Where is it coming from? Retching, you cast your eyes upward and realize that the sound filling your years, your heart and your very soul is being sung by the moon herself. Succumbing to her siren song, you feel your body twist and contort. Strong legs become spindly and gentle. Hands like vice grips become hardened hooves and your face elongates. Finally, a handsome rack of fresh antlers sprout from your skull.

The transformation is complete and the curse has been passed on. Mindless and heeding only the clarion call of Lady Luna herself, you nimbly dart off into the woods to hunt your prey or probably just eat some clover or something.

THE END.

Well, shit. You're sure that you've been possessed by a daemon, but you don't really have a whole lot of options in the way of figuring out what's going on, so you hope it's not a Lying Daemon and decide to ask a few more questions.

Empires come and go, so you don't bother asking any more about where you are. But this word the daemon used to describe you... cyborg. Something about this rings true, so you decide to continue along this line of questioning and get an immediate response.

[QUERY] CYBORG: ONE WHOSE PHYSIOLOGICAL FUNCTIONING IS AIDED OR DEPENDENT ON MECHANICAL OR ELECTRONIC DEVICE. CYB(ernetic) ORG(anism).

Of course, you don't know what mechanical or technological devices are, being a barbarian from a time untold, so you continue to ask more questions. The voice in your head complies and after a few hours of questioning, you've discovered that moments before your impending death, you were rescued by time travelers who, in an attempt to rewrite their shitty post-apocalyptic timeline, traversed the timestream to find a legendary warrior – you! Unfortunately, you were half dead, but they had the ability to transform you into a man/machine hybrid to wage war against the alien invaders who had ravaged their world!

What the fuck?

Anyway, they were successful in repelling the alien invasion, but the human race was pretty much wiped out and with no one left to continue regular maintenance, your reprogramming defaulted and the memories of your former life returned as your own personality reawakened.

Or maybe it's a daemon and it's totally full of shit. But you've always trusted your gut, whether it be full of robot parts and gears, or actual human guts. And your gut tells you this is the truth.

It also tells you to turn to page 7.

Well, its pretty clear at this point that Klaus has good reason to keep his trap shut and you probably should've followed suit. As it is, you've got a flock of peacocks, grouse and other birds closing in on you and they look none too happy.

"Do these reindeer still have any get up n' go, old man?" you ask Klaus.

"Just you wait and see, whippersnapper!" he replies with a gleam in his eye. "Hold on to your britches!"

And with that, he racks the reins. The caribou duo acknowledge and pick up their speed, but the birds are close behind. Dunder and Blixem continue their acceleration, reaching a land speed record heretofore unimaginable. Still, the birds remain right on your tail – a quick look behind you reveals a blackened horizon and a sky nearly blotted out by flapping wings. Klaus continues to urge the reindeer onward with a crazed look in his eye. You begin to question the old man's sanity and again wonder if you might be better off making a hasty exit.

"Reach into the back and grab my satchel!" the old man commands. "I have a plan!"

Do you listen to Klaus and do as you're told? Turn to page 98.

Fuck that. You should've ditched this guy long ago. Turn to page 47 to jump out of this ramshackle death cart.

"Fuck this shit!" you cry as you leap into battle with nary a glance toward your erstwhile companion or a care for your own well-being. You have been known by many names and called a great many things over the years, but those who know you best have said that your propensity for inconsistency is the only consistent thing about you. In matters of the Scissorwulf, no changes are permanent; but change is.

So it is that in spite of the good sense which had earlier prevented you from challenging a wizard, you showed no such acumen when standing face to face with a god (or would-be god, but now is not the time to haggle over semantics). And so it was that you rush headlong into battle with the ferocity of a manticore. But the apoplexy of an earth-bound beast is but a drop in the bucket when compared to the sound and fury of all the birds pf the sky.

The King of Birds remaines still, save for a single finger wagging gently in a "no-no" motion on the end of an outstretched arm as a hundred million birds fly in every direction, obscuring your view and preventing you from making any sort of progress. Their incessant chirping, cawing and crowing is like the tolling of the death knell... and the bell tolls for thee!

Soon, all that is left of you is the bloodied skeleton of a once proud warrior who let his ego and thirst for blood get the better of him. What became of Klaus, the Widowmaker or the King of Birds are mysteries lost to the sands of time. And what of the unicorn horns which were the cause of this whole affair? Ne'er did you learn the whys and wherefores of that puzzlement either.

You know nothing now but the cold and eternal night.

Because you are dead.

THE END.

Nervously, you fake a yawn and stretch your arms.

"Well uh, I'd better turn in," you remark, "we've got a long day ahead of us and we still haven't even discussed what the deal is with that sack of magic horns."

A look of confusion passes across Ghastly Carol's face as she leads you to the ship's hold dejectedly. You were sure you'd seen some empty rooms that you could've slept in, but there must've been some other need for them. Instead, you'll make do with a pile of hay and a bunch of goats and pigs for bedmates.

Carol shakes her head and leaves you with a sigh. You begin to question your choice, but it's too little, too late now. And you were probably just mistaken anyway. You try to convince yourself that you're tired, what with all the slaying and battling that has gone on today.

But you've always had trouble sleeping in a strange place and the day's violence has given rise to your blood and a stirring in your loins. The stench of the animals is foul, but not so much that you are unable to give a coat of polish to your sword, in a manner of speaking. Your spent seed collects in the hay along with a variety of animal excrement and rotten food. Falling quickly into slumber, you dream deeply of one-eyed lady pirates.

Late that evening, as the Lady Fingerle's Revenge casts out for dark waters, an octopus attacks the ship along with a flock of deadly sharks and everyone dies.

THE END.

As a thief, this character must be at least somewhat vile; especially if they're the type of thief who would thieve a sack full of unicorn horns from two other thieves in a filthy tavern in a city as rancorous as Gran'daven. Therefore, they must have taken the path to the left, as the left hand path is the path of evil. Sound logic, if ever such a thing existed.

So you take the path to the left, which immediately becomes darker as all access to city streets or manhole covers is gone. You're walking on a steady decline and struggle to remain upright as the now knee-deep bilge water is running downstream at a fairly steady pace. You soon find yourself trudging through sludge in a cavern as dark as pitch and wonder how many miles beneath the surface you must be or if the thief has even gone this way when suddenly the ground gives out under you!

You're falling fast, but your instincts tell you that the walls of this pit are close – with any luck, you can direct your descent and grab hold of the side of this chasm. But the shock of such a sudden stop could rip even your powerful and sinewy arm right out of its socket. Do you dare take the risk?

Honestly, what other choice do you have? Turn to page 75.

Nay, let us see what is at the bottom. You'll likely hit the river and find the thief! Turn to page 118.

It takes a supreme effort to reach into the back of this rickety old cart as it rolls over rough terrain at such a breakneck speed. But it's a lot easier than the alternative. You've never faced a flock of evil birds yourself, but you've seen their handiwork. Birds tend to go for the eyeballs first, leaving their victims blind as they devour the ears, then the genitals and finally the fingers and toes. It is not a fate you wish to experience firsthand.

Your probing fingers finally discover the worn leather sack carried by Ookla and Thaarl. Handing the bag over to Klaus in exchange for the reins, you realize just how fast the world is going by around you. The trees lining the edges of the worn trail whiz by in a blur of greens and browns. The wind rushes past your face as Klaus thrusts a wrinkled hand into the old sack and produces that which brought you to the dance in the first place – the mythical horn of the horny horse itself – the unicorn's fabled antler!

"Take my hand!" Klaus shouts at you. You're not so sure though, as you've seen what sort of magic Klaus works with his hands. Additionally, and perhaps more importantly, do you really want to hold hands with a dude?

Shall you do as you are instructed and turn to page 51?

You ain't no queer! Turn to page 23.

If you are to die this day, and you most likely are, then let it be with pride. With honor. With a beautiful woman by your side and your sword in your hand. This is your vow as you leap from the dinghy onto the giant head of the Cocktopus to seek vengeance for your lady love and her crew.

The siren song of the Widowmaker rings into the night and it is a sweet song of blood and steel. 'Tis a pity none shall recall it save the light of the gibbous moon, swollen like an expectant mother hanging in the shrouded curtain of night.

The combined might of your deadly prowess and bladework ends the Cocktopus that night, but the injuries you incur in doing so leave both you and Ghastly Carol in no shape to save yourselves. As you lay atop the slowly sinking carcass of the Cocktopus, the sun rises and Carol confides in you.

"Twas a smuggling errand I was on when we met," she explains, "a job from a collector of rare antiquities and treasures. He wasn't even a wizard or one trained in the dark arts; he just kept this stuff on a shelf to admire, I suppose. I took no pride in the job, only a paycheck. I expected to be paid handsomely. I never expected to find love."

A sweet sentiment, but it matters naught, for your time has come. Your fingers intertwine as you witness the arrival of the Refyries, the blind warrior maidens clad in ebony and alabaster who arrive astride winged zebras. It is they who sit in judgment of the merits of a warrior's life. And it is they who raise the hands of the champions as they escort them to the mead halls in the glorious Garden of Grappleheim, where you and Ghastly Carol will reside for all of eternity, drinking until you get your fill.

THE END.

You watch as Klaus' severed head falls to the earth miles beneath you, leaving a faint spray of blood in its wake. His last words echo from his chattering teeth as he falls –

"MOTHERFUCKERRRRRRRRRRRRRRRRrrrrrrrr ... !!!"

You are safe. The reindeer seem docile and despite the loss of their master, they (and the sleigh you're sitting in) aren't following Klaus' head to the ground below.

"Now what?" you ask no one in particular as you slump into the seat, pondering your next move.

"Well, shit!" a voice proclaims, "I say we head home, rustle us up some o' that sacred herb y'all are always getting' on about, get our drink on and find us some lady reindeer to dip our wicks in!"

"Oh hell yes!" a second voice agrees. And at that moment, you realize that you are accompanied by some talking reindeer who are ready to get down.

"So what's your story?" says the reindeer on the left, who you're pretty sure is Blixem. "You like to party?"

Indeed you do. Turn to page 36 and let the merriment begin!

Maybe you should just head home and get some sleep. Turn to page 104.

Fuck it. You've survived against seemingly impossible odds in the past and beyond that, you've never been one to run away or beg another for help. You'll handle this situation as you would any other – by the indomitable strength of your steel.

Like the indiscriminate song of the morning dove, she sang to you from far beneath the earth. Long thought lost by the warrior clans and chronomancers, the Widowmaker called to you as she had to so many champions of prior eras. Just as the Seers of Anon had told you she would when you partook of the sacred herbs in their dark Alkali, where they foretold of futures unwritten and secrets too deadly to keep. Reforged in spellbound fire, her broken shards were more powerful than ever. Thrice cursed by a witch and enraptured by the blessing of a magus, these enchantments worked in conjunction with the mettle in your soul.

As always, you work in tandem, for the Widowmaker serves no master and the Scissorwulf kneels before no weapon, be it mortal or ensorcelled. Hilt in fist. Blade in hand. Meat cut to the bone. Spilt blood, splintered cartilage and shattered dreams are the order of the day and soldiers from both armies meet their end at the edge of your sword as you carve a path through the battlefield to make your escape.

But unbeknownst to anyone, this war is waged too near the sacred cave of Golarr, an ancient monster worm who has slumbered in his fleshy chrysalis since before man walked upright. And at that exact moment, he emerges, no longer a pupa but a full-grown iron butterfly – one who breathes the flames of vengeance from deep within his gullet. He awakens in anger and carries that rage onto the battlefield, burning all to a crisp before delivering that same fate unto the rest of the earth, until naught was left but embers.

THE END.

A man with better judgment might still his tongue, but while you have born witness to many an oddity and emerged triumphant from many trials of life, your tongue is like the chicken – quick to run and with little thought propelling it.

"I am a hunter," you reply and, gesturing toward Ookla and Thaarl, "these men are my prey." A bold statement, to be sure, but something in the air has emboldened you this day.

You remain still as Ghastly Carol slowly circles you, her singular eye studying every muscled inch of your body. After what feels like an eternity, she stops directly in front of you and finally speaks.

"So tell me hunter, what is it that drives you to pursue such prey? Do you hunt for sustenance or merely the thrill that comes with the kill?" Her fingers dance lightly upon the hilt of her sword as she speaks and you know that you must choose your next words wisely, lest they be your last. As a man who has always attempted to walk the path of truth, you decide that it will serve you well yet again.

"Neither," you reply, "I hunt for justice."

Ghastly Carol's eyebrows rise at your response.

"Very well then, hunter. Join me on my quest and we shall hunt as a pack!"

It would seem that in this adventure, you have no choice but to turn to page 62.

The Doler of Justice. The shadow who lurks in the darkened doorway. The Keeper of the Extinguished Flame. You have been called by many names, but quitter has never been one of them. You are the Scissorwulf, illegitimate son of a god, your mother's mortal womb was the only one that could bear his seed. You who are your own spirit animal. You who found the crossing at the Golden Rainbow's end. You do not simply *give up*.

So you travel the scorched earth, your rotting flesh animated by the power of the sub-nuclear cell battery contained in the power source within your metal ribcage, your plexisteel and kineti-craft pistons propelling you through this ravaged world. Centuries pass and still you walk.

The radiation which has ruined this world subsides and life begins anew. Once again, the world is green, as it was said to be in the legends of the early days. Quite by chance, you stumble upon the Widowmaker, secreted away in an underground cave miles beneath the earth. Whole again, your journey continues.

And there comes a day when an alien spacefaring vessel arrives, its hyperspace motivator damaged. Using your internal power source and the magic of your enchanted blade, you salvage their ship and allow them the opportunity to return home. Joining these spacefarers, you aid in the defeat of the intergalactic warlord who had subjugated their people for so many years.

For this, you are granted a kingdom on one of the small moons of their homeworld. But the burden of a crown never suited you the way a battlefield did. Graciously declining, you leave to join an interstellar professional wrestling organization where you reign as champion until suffering a career ending injury at the hands of Neblurious Prime.

Your physical form ravaged and rendered useless, you upload your computer-driven brain into a sentient spaceship and continue to travel the highways of the universe to this very day.

THE END.

You're thankful for the gesture, but a bit rattled by the experience, so instead of partying, you just ask the reindeer to take you back into town and drop you off. It's a bold faced lie and everyone knows it. An awkward silence accompanies your ride back to Gran'daven, which totally sucks because you're dying to know what the deal is with Klaus and those birds and the unicorn horns.

Alas, you'll never know. Dunder and Blixem drop you off a mile or so outside of town, as it serves no cause for a talking animal to venture too close to civilization, where superstitious folk might cause them harm.

"We'll take care of these." Dunders says of the sack of unicorn horns. "But why don't you take one for yourself, in case you feel so inclined."

You nod in agreement and take a horn. It doesn't take long for you to walk into town and secure food, drink and companionship from a local whore. Later that evening, after food, drink and woman have been imbibed, you find yourself weary but unable to sleep. Holding the severed unicorn horn in your hand, your thoughts travel on the winds of magic, transmitted to Dunder and Blixem via the power of unicorn power.

"'Sup, dude?" a bleary-eyed Blixem asks, "You still wanna party?"

You nod in agreement and within the hour, find yourself back in the sleigh on a harrowing ride toward a darkened part of the forest where your reindeer friends have set up a small camp. No doubt, this will be some enchanted evening.

Turn thineself to page 36.

By now, the pain is absolutely unbearable, so you turn your attention away from the briny beast to the tiny demons engorging themselves on your nether regions. Or, what was left of them – you'd be surprised what a mermonkey can fit it its mouth.

Just then, you hear a resounding CRACK and realize that the Cocktopus has been successful. Lady Fingerle's Revenge has been rent in two, torn asunder by this undersea monstrosity. A quick glance shows that any surviving crewmember is either engaged in the act of drowning or fending off several mermonkeys. And what of Ghastly Carol? How ironic that fate should, on the very same day, give unto you a woman whom you might truly love and could love you in return only to snatch her away from you with an army of amphibious fiends? You might have taken a moment to appreciate the cruel joke, if your mutilated genitals weren't throbbing in agony.

Just as the ship begins to capsize and you no longer have the strength to continue fighting the swarms of mermonkeys, you hear a scream! It is none other than the voice of your lady love, Ghastly Carol!

Shall you attempt to fight on in order to save her? Turn to page 34 to do so.

Fuck it – you're dead in the water. Just give in, give up and get thineself to page 16.

No sooner do the words escape your mouth do you find yourself on your back with the scourge of the high seas upon you, desperately removing the small piece of cloth which separates her lustful rose from your engorged and throbbing manhood. It seems that luck will indeed be a lady tonight!

Setting forth on this carnal path, it feels as though the thrusting and grinding of two such passionate spirits would set the very earth to tremble in your wake. Then you realize that indeed, the ground beneath you does quake! It is an earth tremor, the kind which had sunk the proud city of Catlantis nary a decade prior!

Cursing the gods who would deny you the full knowledge of Ghastly Carol's body and soul, you share one last embrace with perhaps the only woman who is your equal in matters of both love and war. The earth opens up and swallows the two of you, the tavern which bears witness to the exquisiteness of your sin and indeed, the entire city of Gran'daven.

As you fall into the endless black, a scream of pleasure and anger is in your throat. For this is...

The End.

Ghastly Carol's crew is a bone to be chewed and if they notice that you are completely nude as you fight off the hordes of invading mermonkeys, they see no reason to give mention to it. Within seconds, the compliment of 125 are outnumbered by the nocturnal marauders. Though the creatures are easy enough to kill, with each death, it seemed that two more arose to take their place. The tiny creatures are tearing the ship apart with hands and teeth and interrupting their frenzy only ensures their rage will then be directed upon you. The deck is soon littered with bodies, both human and aqua-primate.

You have no time to think. No time to reflect upon unicorn-related mysteries or the reason you're on this ship, save to make sweet, sweet love to Ghastly Carol. Is it the thought of her or the thrill of the battle that puts your own ship at half mast as the Lady Fingerle's Revenge is being destroyed all around you? The spill of blood does seem to have such an effect on a warrior such as yourself.

That effect was not lost on your lover either, who bravely fights beside you against the ever increasing foes. Stealing a glance at your enlarged member, she comments,

"Aye, there is nothing like carnage to dampen a maiden's nethers and I swear to you that when this battle is done, we'll resume the passions we left behind in the boudoir. But for now, there is much work to be done!"

And then the other shoe drops. Turn to page 89.

"Come now, Klaus," you gently chastise your travelling companion, clearly forgetting your teachings at the feet of Elijah, chancellor of the Temple of Ma'twelzian Monks, "Surely mere *birds* pose no threat to us!"

The words have scarcely been spoken when the path before you is blocked by a gathering of wings and feathers the likes of which you've never seen. Within seconds, the cart is surrounded by birds of all types. Their sole purpose is carnage, and moments later they have cleaned the reindeer of all flesh and muscle and even managed to completely disassemble the cart you'd been riding in, which is really pretty impressive considering the fact that they aren't using any tools or anything.

Your eyes wide and mouth agape, you watch as the birds form a swirling mass. Slowly, the mass of airfoil, crest and pinion take shape, forming a splendid cloak of feathers which, when swept back, reveals none other than the King of Birds himself!

The ruler of the Kingdom of the Air, the illustrious King of Birds knows all and hears even more. The subject of many a legend, it is said that he was once a man who achieved godhood through his friendship with all winged creatures, who fetch secrets and information for him through a vast network of conspirators. But the knowledge he has gained has driven him mad. He stands before you, resplendent in his plumage, while dozens of birds flit about.

Shall you lay waste to him, as you have so many others? Turn to page 95.

Maaaaaayyyybe that's not such a good idea? Instead, focus your attentions on page 122.

Though nary a drop of giant's blood runs through your veins, there are those who have questioned if you are, in fact, of their ilk. For surely your enormous appetite for love, justice, vengeance and especially the sacred herbs rival the icy proclivities of those who can move mountains. A bold man with even bolder tastes, your thirst for knowledge is as great as your thirst for blood. A big man with a big heart, you live life to the biggest. So it goes without saying that your instinct is to imbibe as though you were partying with the gods themselves.

Perhaps it is something in the air or just the strange nature of the night's events, but something tells you to hold off tonight. And as always, your instincts hold true. For a shift in the wind and the snap of a dry leaf alert your keenly honed senses to a potential danger.

Is it a third member of the thieves' guild? Perhaps a wild animal ravenous for its next meal? Surely there is no time to ponder – your next move could prove your last!

Shall you lay in wait, ready to spring a trap upon whom – or *what*ever awaits you in the wood? Turn to page 70.

Or will you run, hoping to outrun the lurker in the darkness? Turn to page 81.

Rejuvenated by the healing power of the unicorn's sacred horn, you are wide awake as Ghastly Carol tells her tale and the night becomes day. She speaks of a life of piracy, as is the way of the Altazzarrians, and of many treasures plundered. She speaks of one final score: the big job which every sensible thief and brigand dreams of. The job with a payout so large, one can retire from thieving and leave the high seas behind so that the remainder of one's days may be lived like a blade of grass on one's own personal island. To live the life of a pirate and not plan for the big job is simply irresponsible. This job – to retrieve a worn leather satchel from two rogues and transport it by sea to a contact in De'twaa with no questions asked – this was to be that job.

But Ghastly Carol hadn't counted on the mermonkeys and she hadn't counted on the Coctopus. She certainly hadn't counted on falling in love.

And now? Well, she had her own private island and she had someone with whom to spend the rest of her days. As unlikely to discover the truth about her employer as you are to survive more than a fortnight on this deserted island, you are thankful for each other and you are thankful for the last remaining unicorn horn. This island seems devoid of vegetation or wildlife, but there are rocks. And rocks can be used to grind that antler into powder.

You'll both be dead within the month, but you'll have one hell of a party in the meantime.

THE END.

111

Though it is not in your nature to be confined, nor to remain in a room where you had been once been shackled, you begin to explore your erstwhile cell. In mere moments, the symbols on the strange glass which cover the walls begin to make sense. Though you feel a pins-and-needles sensation in your extremities, it quickly gives way to a renewed sense of strength. Your body feels full of vigor, not at all the way it felt when the mermonkeys had...

Wait! Hadn't the mermonkeys devoured your toes and fingers? Hadn't they flayed the flesh from your body? Raising your hands in front of you, a shock runs to the very core of your being. Your hands are restored – wholly intact, but transformed (a voice in your head corrects you: REPLACED) into a strange flexible metal. A cursory glance reveals that your legs too are no longer flesh, but the same arcane metal. What manner of alchemy allows the same steel used to make armor and blade to bend as though it were muscle or sinew? What type of wizard could achieve such a feat of magic?

You get your answer as a voice echoes throughout the chamber – or was it just inside your head?

"Hello, Agent Scissorwulf!" the voice says in an unfamiliar accent. "How do you like your new body?"

What's all this, then? Turn to page 17 to find out!

"Fuck that asshole." you say in reply to the question posed by the King of Birds. "He was just some creepy pervert wizard I was tailing to find out what the deal was with the unicorn horns. For I am the Scissorwulf, friend of nature and Doler of Justice! I sought an answer to my question and a quest to right the wrong that has been perpetrated against these once proud animals."

The King of Birds responds, "Then consider your quest complete, my friend, for Klaus was but a pawn in my game! The unicorn's antler was the last piece of the mystical puzzle I was attempting to solve in order to further my own cause."

"And now, coupled with the Rosary of Sorrows," he says, pointing at the beaded necklace which ringed his collarbones, "and the Tabernacle of Endowment," he continues while producing a tiny golden box from within the shrouds of his majestic cloak of feathers, "I now have a complete set!"

Giddy and crazed with glee, his royal aviary went on,

"The Power Eternal is now mine and I shall take my rightful place among the Titans of Grappleheim, seated at the right hand of Victorious King Mayhem!"

With these words comes a great many squawkings, cackles and titters from the dozens of birds which surround the area, followed by a crack of thunder and a bolt of lightning. Shit is about to go get real.

RUN! Turn to page 61!

Fuck this motherfucker! Turn to page 90.

Though your body feels numb, you focus all of your energy toward the light, willing it nearer. Shockingly, it seems to be working, as the brilliant white luminescence grows closer... closer still. A sense of calm snuggles you like a warm puppy, filling you with peace as the light grows more intense, threatening to overtake the dark.

You've heard tales of a man's life passing before his eyes as he makes his way beyond the veil to the great drinking halls in the Garden of Grappleheim – an account of battles won and lost, lovers loved and friend and foe alike. A grand recounting so that the tales may be fresh in one's mind to share around the table as bread and mead are consumed until the sands of time run out. But it is not so for you; all you see is light. All memory is forgotten and only the light remains. The all-consuming light, which removes doubt and fear...

And now there is no dark. There is no thought. No question; only the light. Your sense of time and even your sense of self fades away as you become one with the light.

And then you wake up. But that won't happen until you turn to page 35.

You find yourself surrounded now by a pack of wild dogs. Judging by their mangy hides and exposed ribs, these beasts hunger for meat and have plans to make a meal of you!

As first dog lunges, you instinctively bring your arm up to protect yourself. You are shocked to find that the dog's teeth shatter as they wrap around your forearm. Whatever it is you're made of, it is powerful indeed! Two more dogs meet the same fate, but the one that sneaks up behind finds a tender spot at the small of your back. Whatever type of monstrosity you've become, *that* part of you is still human.

After wrestling the final canine into submission, you snap its neck for good measure. Without thinking, you quickly do the same to the rest of them before they can flee. It's as though you are no longer in control of your own body. Again, unfamiliar symbols forming an alien word flash before your eyes:

[PRIME DIRECTIVE: CONTINUED SURVIVAL]

You continue to search the devastated ruins of this once proud kingdom, finding nothing but battered remains of a long dead civilization and deadly wild animals, the likes of which you've never seen. You begin to feel an urge to continue; as though you are being led somewhere. In time, your path leads you right back to where you started.

Something is drawing you here. Clearly the answers you seek are inside. Turn to page 84.

That's stupid. Turn to page 60 to find shelter elsewhere.

Fuck that shit. You don't take orders from nobody, especially some bird freak. Then again, you've been on a journey in a rickety old cart with a creepy old wizard who fondles himself in order to perform magic. Maybe this is the guy you *should* trust?

But it's too late. Klaus has already withdrawn a unicorn horn from his sack and hurled it at the King of Birds, piercing him through his heart. No blood drips from the wound, which emanates a pure, blinding light. So blinding that it blinds you!

You can't be sure what happens next, but it definitely involves birds, scuffling and a lot of curses. Torrential rains batter your body as Klaus and the King of Birds do battle. And maybe an earthquake? You can't be too sure, because you are blind and once the ground gives way, you pretty much just die instantly.

Who ended up with the unicorn horns? Why did they even want them anyway? You don't know, and you'll never know because you made poor choices and you died.

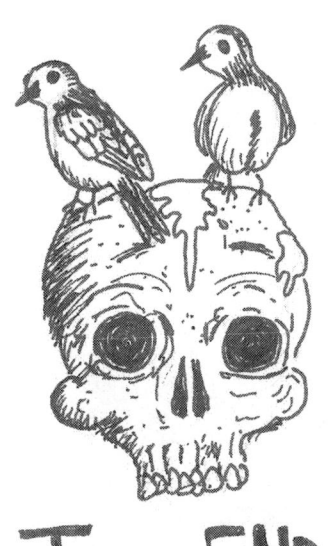

THE END.

Disconnected from your corporeal form, tales of days gone by play out before you like a stage production. You bear witness to a king among gods as he assumes the form of a grand peacock so that he might inveigle a mortal woman who had caught his eye and captured his heart, however briefly.

You then see a babe in swaddling clothes, already a pariah by virtue of his lineage, cast out of a small hamlet after his mother died in childbirth. A congregation of elders take the child in and, as is the custom of their tribe, consult the sacred herbs to determine the child's spirit animal and thus, his name.

But what of the child whose namesake is his own? Educated in the ways of the earth and spirit by a family of bears and raised to walk the path of the warrior by a lonely sharecropper who had once been a general in the Royal Guard before falling victim to drink.

As the illusion continues, the visions come faster and more frenzied... a struggle with a shapeshifter... the loss of a friend... the siren song of the Widowmaker, which called to you at night... the reforging of that ancient sword... a cornucopia of lovers who taught the lad the arts of amour... and battles. So many battles; for honor, pride and justice.

Finally, the visions come faster and faster until they are naught but a blur of light and fury. And then...

TURN TO PAGE 73.

The sewers of Gran'daven are the most obvious and easiest escape route frequented by the underclass – you've used them yourself on occasion. But this thief is no common rogue; they've displayed an uncanny intellect which leads you to believe they'll take a far more surreptitious path by simply hiding in plain sight and bleeding in with the crowds in the manner of the Tsarevna frog.

Using an apple cart as a launch point, you leap onto the colorful canopy of a nearby brothel which propels you up onto a rooftop. From here, you have a clear view of the city streets. Treacherous this thief may be, but you've been trained in the art of the hunt by no less than The Venturian himself and very little escapes your keen eye.

Just then, you spot the sleek velour cloak of the thief moving through the throng as a shark moves through the sea. A proud warrior, you know your skill level just as surely as you know the deadly steel slumbering upon your back. Following and apprehending the thief would be child's play, but it could be tricky due to the number of citizens nearby. And who knows if the burglar has compatriots? You could just as easily heave the Widowmaker, skewer the larcenist and end this now.

Will you give chase? Turn to page 128.

Shall you let the pilferer know the gentle caress of steel? Turn to page 63.

You surmise that the chasm likely ends at the Remulite River and therefore the safest option is to simply fall. You stretch your body into a dive so that you can cut the water like a knife, ensuring that the fall will not result in injury.

And as unlikely as it seems, your plan works! Your fall ends in a body of water with seemingly no bottom. You slice though the lymph like a hot blade through butter incurring no injuries. Quickly rising to the surface, you catch one last gasp of air before the piranha attack. Dozens, perhaps hundreds of them strike at once, nibbling and gnawing at every available piece of flesh. You've heard tell that these hungry little man-eaters can take a grown man down to naught but bone in less than 30 seconds.

Fortunately for you, it only takes 15.

The way of the thief is the left hand path. Simple logic dictates that one who would practice the craft of banditry would, by nature of their being, follow the tunnel to the left. But a larcenist so audacious as to burgle a bag of enchanted antlers – one so vile as to take part in an action that spits in the face of Mother Nature and could rob the world of magic – would be too intelligent to do what is expected. They would know that any hunter with the skill to track them this far would possess an equally keen intellect. Therefore and thus being, said thief would be likely to take the tunnel on the right.

Also, you've noticed in the dim light that the right path is devoid of cobwebbery, while the left remains untouched and full of spider's silk. You could've very well skipped all of that deduction and explanation earlier on the page, but working it all out in your head is just part of your process.

Thankful that you won't have to traverse the cobweb-filled tunnel, you make your way down the ever-darkening corridor on the right. After several yards, you come to an open room with but two exits: a small window on the other side of the room, approximately 12 feet above the floor, and the door behind you from whence you hear the heavy, labored breathing of what can only be a hideous beast.

Turn to page 126 to make a run for the window.

Turn to page 52 if fighting is more your style.

120

Having obtained the answers you need, you call upon your all-too-brief training with the Ma'twelzian Monks on the steppes of the Mystic Mountains and speak the most magical word you know.

"COZUMBA!"

In a flash of light, the daemon is trapped within your enchanted blade and the world around you reverts to normal. You find yourself surrounded by forest, still bereft of clothing or sustenance. Two dilemmas easily rectified by a hunt – you are in the woods after all.

But the quandary vexing you now is not a physical one. Nay, it is a matter of the heart that brings pain to the heart of the Scissorwulf. You cannot be sure how much of your recent adventure was real and how much was daemon-induced dream, but the longing you feel for Ghastly Carol haunts you like a phantom dove. You know that she is out there somewhere and you will not rest until you are reunited. Or perhaps united for the first time if it turns out that everything has just been a dream.

One quest ends and another begins. Such is the life of the warrior born. And in this adventure, you know that you have no choice. You must follow your heart down whatever path it leads, until you find she who fills up your senses like a night in the forest.

THE END... for now.

"That bitch is crazy!" you mutter to yourself as you start rowing away from the scene of the slaughter. Ghastly Carol remains atop the brow of the Cocktopus, hacking away and managing to put out the creature's left eye. In her rage, it has not occurred to her that in killing the killer that killed her crew, she will also be killing herself. You recall tales of the madness which afflicts those who are out at sea too long and row harder.

A great many mysteries will be left unanswered, with only the dark and churning sea and the light of the gibbous moon to bear witness. The tragic death of the Scissorwulf will be among them, as the thrashing of the Cocktopus' mighty tentacles cause wave after wave to pummel and punish your tiny craft. Fast as you are, not even the rippling sinew of your brawny thews are enough to create fair distance to save your life.

Your lungs filling with seawater, the last sight you see is that of the Refyries - the blind warrior maidens who sit in judgment of those who die in combat. Clad in onyx and ivory, they swoop in on flying zebras to carry the fallen warriors off to the mead halls in the Gardens of Grappleheim. But today, they come only for Ghastly Carol, not you. For today, the Scissorwulf, formerly known as the Doler of Justice, is known only … as coward.

THE END.

Be they man, wizard or would-be-god, you know when you are outmatched. Despite a lifelong history of thick headedness and foolhardy decisions, your momma didn't raise no fool.

Actually, you never knew your mother, who had died in childbirth. The victim of cruel fate, her legendary beauty had led her to become lover to a god, though her mortal womb would prove too weak to carry the burden of divine seed. At any rate, a poor sharecropper had found a swaddling babe in the field and had taken it in. As the babe grew, the sharecropper taught you him the mysteries of the earth and the Way of the Warrior (for he had been a soldier in the Royal Guard before drink got the better of him). He lessons instilled within you a levelheadedness and acumen that had served you well. And it was that good sense which told you not to fuck with the man who holds sway over every flying thing in the world.

Proud as a peacock, the King of Birds stands before you, neither moving nor speaking for what feels like an eternity. Finally...

"Behold! Your true enemy stands before you! It is Klaus who is the evil mastermind in this scheme! Destroy him now, before it is too late!"

The King of Birds hath spoken and laid down his commands. But do you believe him?

Yeah, he seems to be on the level. Turn to page 27.

Fuck that noise. Turn to page 115.

The darkness is all consuming and you welcome its inky embrace. But as you surrender yourself to Parts Unknown, that pinprick of light grows ever brighter... and brighter still. Though you have chosen the dark, the light seeks you and it will not be denied!

Gazing into it, you allow the light to surround and caress you. Soon, you can see little else, but in a moment's time, a face begins to emerge from the whiteness. It is Ghastly Carol, who swims toward you, carrying a unicorn's horn aloft in her hand like a torch. The horn glows like a beacon, cutting through the night like a sword through a child's tender spine (not that you have any concept of what that would be like; but you've been told). Offering the antler to you, she commands – "Take hold!"

Somehow, you manage to find enough strength to swim toward your lover. Taking her hand, you feel the rejuvenating force of the unicorn's horn work it's magic on your body, replenishing you and healing your wounds. As the two of you swim away from the wreckage, your body is made whole once more. Swimming for what feels like hours, you leave behind the slaughtered crew and find yourself on a deserted island.

"We have much to discuss," says Ghastly Carol.

'bout fucking time! Turn to page 110.

"Fuck this shit," you mutter under your breath as you grit your teeth and tighten your grip on the Widowmaker's handle. Your mind is finally clear. You are free from the daemon's influence and ready to end this battle.

Your first attempt is unsuccessful. Lunging at the creature, it easily sidesteps you and sends you sprawling in the dirt. As you fall, the daemon slaps you on your naked hindquarters – a warning of what is to come, should you fail to win this day.

Propping yourself up on your elbows, you are primed to rejoin the battle, but the daemon has primed its pump for something else. Before you have even a moment to breathe, it is upon you like a wolverine in heat. An exquisite pain fills your hands as you realize they are pinned to the earth, a unicorn's severed horn piercing each one! You cannot move and as the foul beast begins its assault, it whispers in your ear. There are not the sweet nothings and tenderness of a lover, but the tale of a creature banished from the lofty heights of the gods and forced to traverse the realms of mortals in an immaterial form until it can find a new host and reproduce.

Asbjorn was its name and it had manipulated the thieves and even the game hunters who had trafficked in the unicorn's horn. It had called upon a favor from the Lords of the Deep to unleash the mermonkeys and the Cocktopus to bring ruin upon The Lady Fingerle's Revenge and now it makes ruin of your chocolate starfish and unleashes into your rectal cavity.

For more excitement, look no further than page 24.

Reflecting upon the net which holds you, you recall that the spider waits patiently all day, knowing what it will gain. Though great satisfaction would be found by ending the lives of your captors, it would bring you no closer to solving the mystery and learning who the greater evil of this story is. And so, you wait.

Sitting cross-legged on the forest floor, the minutes turn into hours and you still your mind and body, reaching a deep meditative state. Underestimating the power of the poison your captors have utilized, you relax to the point of intoxication and finally, lose consciousness.

You awaken to the rising of the sun and the arrival of a new dawn. Still numb from the sedative, you are shocked to find yourself upright, several feet from the ground. A large golden spike pierces each of your wrists and your ankles, pinning you to some manner of enormous, cross-shaped symbol. Your captors surround you, their naked bodies bathed in the light of the new day. In their hands are the stolen unicorn horns, which glow brighter with each hideous chant of an ancient and long unheard language that escapes from their tongues.

Fear begins to overwhelm you as you struggle to maintain your sanity. The cultists take turns piercing your stomach and undercarriage with the horns and you watch your innards spill out onto the dew covered grass, thankful that the poison in your body keeps the pain at bay.

But when the ground upon which your blood has been spilt erupts and you look upon the face of the daemon which your sacrifice has brought forth, there is nothing left for you to do but scream.

THE END.

It takes but four strides to reach the other side of the dark room and launch yourself upward to the narrow window on the other side. But it is still not fast enough to escape the monstrosity which hunts you. At the very moment your hand grasps the window's sill, you feel gigantic claws wrap around your midsection, piercing your skin and crushing your ribcage.

You never do get a good look at this foul creature, for it is as efficient as it is rancid. No doubt it has lurked in these dank catacombs for years, feasting upon the unsuspecting transients and criminals who traverse the labyrinth, for it has grown to a massive size; a cyclopean mass of fur, claws, tentacles and teeth, all of which work in conjunction to rend, tear and gnaw you to pieces.

Soon, you are little more than a splash of blood upon the walls and floor, the better part of you is being digested in the beasts' corpulent belly, to be shat out in several days time.

Ashes to ashes, dust to dust.

Your lips twist into a smile as you consider the hideous beast before you. It has eliminated the thief who attempted to steal away with the satchel full of unicorn antlers. And though it hampers your investigation into the matter and has trapped you in its kill room, this simple act of nature makes the creature a sort of kin to you; for in doing what comes naturally, it hath become a Doler of Justice not unlike yourself. One of a kind, like the Scissorwulf, and the Widowmaker. A part of you will be sad to see it destroyed. But only a very small part.

You rush toward the monster, Widowmaker in hand. It rises up on its spindly legs, tentacles thrashing wildly. But the beast is slow, having eaten recently, a position you intend to exploit.

Leaping over and dodging tentacles, you slide under the monster's belly, carving it like a distended haggis. The beasts' innards spill out onto the floor and all over you. Unfortunately, such a creature has within its digestive tract stomach acids so potent that it sears nearly all of the flesh from your body instantly.

And so it goes. The Widowmaker, forged in the heart of a dragon, carrying the curse of a witches coven and the blessing of a high magus, remains as your epitaph, quietly singing her song of justice until another brave warrior hears and follows.

THE END.

Leaping from rooftop to rooftop, you manage to outpace the rapscallion in mere minutes. Then, using several canopies and flagpoles to slow your descent, you drop down directly in front of the thief, who comes to an abrupt stop, impaled upon the sensuous steel of the Widowmaker's savage blade. Looking you directly in the eyes as she takes her final breath, the thief sputters blood and manages to mutter three prophetic words.

"A ... calculated ... risk ..."

Suddenly, you realize that you are surrounded. The thief hadn't turned down a random street; she had led you into a trap! Dozens of citizens, clad in the same black cloaks as their compatriot, close in on you, striking your person repeatedly with small daggers. You have no room to maneuver. No room to swing your enchanted blade and bring unto your assassins the Widowmaker's deadly gift.

As you fall to the blood soaked earth, you reach out to one of your assailants and grasp the ancient medallion hanging about his neck. You recognize the symbol carved into bronze as that of an ancient cult of serpent worshippers long thought dead. As you breath your last breath, you hear someone whisper...

"The Union of the Snake is on the climb!"

But for you, this is THE END.

Made in the USA
Columbia, SC
07 July 2025